Reading Comprehension
And Rauding Theory

Reading Comprehension And Rauding Theory

By

RONALD P. CARVER, Ph.D.

Professor, Division of Educational Research and Psychology
School of Education
University of Missouri – Kansas City

CHARLES C THOMAS • PUBLISHER
Springfield • Illinois • U.S.A.

Published and Distributed Throughout the World by
CHARLES C THOMAS • PUBLISHER
2600 South First Street
Springfield, Illinois 62717, U.S.A.

© *1981, by* CHARLES C THOMAS • PUBLISHER

ISBN 0-398-04495-3

Library of Congress Catalog Card Number: 81-4925

Library of Congress Cataloging in Publication Data

Carver, Ronald P.
  Reading comprehension and rauding theory.

  Bibliography: p.
  Includes index.
  1. Reading comprehension. I. Title. II. Title:
Rauding theory.
LB1050.45   428.4'3   81-4925
ISBN 0-398-04495-3   AACR2

Printed in the United States of America
C-1

INTRODUCTION

THIS BOOK has been written to explain rauding theory. This theory provides an alternative way of looking at reading and reading comprehension. According to conventional wisdom, good readers are viewed as being flexible; they are continually changing their purpose, and they are continually changing their rate. Rauding theory provides an alternative view of reading that is counter to this continual shifting from one purpose to another. The typical purpose for reading is to communicate with the author of the material by comprehending each thought that the author has written down. In rauding theory, a reader is also pictured as typically having a constant rate of reading, not a continually changing reading rate. This typical purpose and this typical rate are the main ingredients of what may be called "typical reading." When an individual is engaged in typical reading, the person is said to be "rauding." This book contains the principles, laws, and hypotheses that are relevant to rauding. This book quantifies the accuracy of comprehension and the efficiency of comprehension using mathematical formulas.

Rauding theory was first advanced in a lengthy journal article published in the 1977-78 volume of the *Reading Research Quarterly*.[1] That presentation of the theory was evidently very difficult to understand; at least it appears that many of the criticisms of the theory have stemmed from a lack of understanding. One of the purposes of this book is to present rauding theory in a form that is easier to understand. This book contains a rearticulation of the theory, but it is not written in the traditional style of a scholarly article. Instead, it is written in the form of a dialogue between a fictitious graduate student, named Fran, and Professor Carver, the originator of the theory. The student

---

1. Ronald P. Carver, "Toward a Theory of Reading Comprehension and Rauding," *Reading Research Quarterly, 13*:8-63, 1977-78.

Fran, has had trouble understanding the original presentation of the theory and Professor Carver elaborates and responds to questions.

This book is not simply a rehash of the first presentation of rauding theory. The theory was originally presented in the form of hypotheses and generalizations. It stayed close to what could be inferred from existing empirical data with extensive references to the research of others. In contrast, the explanations in this book contain a few references to published research, and the theory is presented from a reasoned standpoint — from the standpoint of rationalism instead of empiricism. In the first part of the book, Part I, there is an attempt to state the principles of the theory, derive laws from principles, and derive hypotheses from laws. Also in Part I, Carver attempts to explain to Fran how the hypotheses of rauding theory have received empirical support; he does this by simplifying and summarizing the results of four research studies.

Part II of the book continues with the dialogue between Carver and Fran. It is assumed in Part II that Fran has read the research relevant to rauding theory and understands the theory fairly well. In this part, Carver responds to criticisms and speculates about the implications of the theory. Rauding theory is related to psycholinguistics, schema theory, reading instruction, and reading research.

Those who raud the entire book should know almost all that is presently known about rauding theory. They should be aware of all the ways in which the theory has been criticized, and they should have their own criticisms. They should be able to see how to design research to test rauding theory. They should also be better able to evaluate any scientific theory, because Carver defends rauding theory using numerous concepts from the philosophy of science and illustrations from the physical sciences. Finally, and most important, they should be able to evaluate whether in fact rauding theory is *viable* as an alternative to the conventional view of reading.

The consequences of accepting rauding theory and rejecting the contemporary view of reading are far-reaching. No longer will it be proper to talk about studying "the reading process," as if there were only one such process. No longer will it be proper to conduct research in reading without making it clear whether or not "rauding" is being investigated. No longer will reading research be simply a qualitative science. Acceptance of rauding theory forces a restructuring of prior knowledge and provides a different structure for creating new knowledge.

ACKNOWLEDGMENTS

Anyone who writes a book is indebted to a great many people. I've had many teachers who helped me through twenty years of schooling. My parents, wife, and children provided me with a milieu conducive to thinking and writing. Secretaries, deans, and fellow faculty members provided institutional support. Government agencies, such as the National Institute of Education, the U.S. Office of Naval Research, and the National Institute of Health, provided the research support necessary for generating the ideas contained in the book. Many researchers have influenced my thinking through their reports; some of these researchers will detect that influence even when there is no direct citation of their work.

Finally, I want to thank those people who were directly involved in reviewing earlier drafts of the manuscript. They can justifiably claim credit for improving the book and can justifiably deny responsibility for its shortcomings. Those people are as follows: James Hoffman, Fred Duffelmeyer, Marilyn Eanet, Martha Haggard, Mark Condon, Robert Leibert, Blanche Sosland, Deanna Martin, Robert Blanc, Ula Casale, Ann Powell-Brown, Joseph Wolff, and George Gale. I also want to thank the typists, Suzan Murphy and Barbara Dorrance.

To Mary Lou
Melanie
Heather

CONTENTS

xi

Reading Comprehension
And Rauding Theory

PART I
WHAT IS RAUDING THEORY?

Chapter 1

WHAT IS RAUDING?

Fran: Professor Carver, I have tried to read your theory of rauding but I have had trouble with it. I want to understand, but it is very complex. Would you mind elaborating on the theory, explaining it again in a simpler way if possible?

Carver: Sure, where would you like for me to start?

Fran: To use a cliché, let's start at the very beginning. What is "rauding"?

Carver: To explain what rauding is, I need to digress for a moment to another subject, the history of science. The early Greeks considered air to be a basic element. This idea stemmed from Aristotle's contention that the four basic elements were earth, air, fire, and water. His idea was that all substances could be analyzed into these four components, that is, everything was formed from combinations of these basic ingredients. These ideas were prevalent for many centuries, up until the time of Lavoisier. There was a quantum leap forward when Lavoisier discovered that air contained something more basic; air was partly composed of a more fundamental ingredient called "oxygen." Since Lavoisier, the separation of air into more primary components such as oxygen, nitrogen, and argon has been very important because this has made it possible to advance our knowledge about each of the components. Science has tended to progress by analyzing things into more fundamental units, such as atoms and molecules. Of course, even today the layperson gets along fine without making these fundamental distinctions — most people couldn't care less that air was composed of 1% argon, for example. However, a scientist in modern times who investigated oxygen and implicitly gave the impression that the results were likely to apply to air in general would be laughed at, to say the least. By analogy, I think many modern reading researchers are very similar to the laypersons who do not discriminate between air and oxygen, or between air and nitrogen.

I think most people in the field of reading are making the mistake of thinking that reading is a fundamental element when there are more basic components of reading that are not being recognized as distinct. I think rauding is a fundamental component of reading just as oxygen is a fundamental component of air. I think skimming, for example, is another fundamental component of reading that is as different from rauding as nitrogen is different from oxygen. I think that the concept of rauding is crucially important for all those people who have more than a layperson's interest in the area of reading. If people in reading, whether researchers or practitioners, do not soon make a distinction between reading in general and rauding in particular, or rauding in particular and skimming in particular, then progress is going to continue to be impeded. Just as progress in chemistry was given a tremendous boost when it was recognized that air was not a fundamental element, I think progress in reading will be given a tremendous boost when it is recognized that reading is not a fundamental element.

Fran: Perhaps it is a bit forward of me to say so, but aren't you extremely optimistic? Isn't it a little grandiose to think that the idea of rauding will do for the field of reading what the idea of oxygen did for the field of chemistry?

Carver: I'll have to agree with you there. To carry the analogy that far would be dreaming. I don't really expect that much of an impact or consequence.

I don't want to procrastinate any further; let me get on with explaining what rauding means.

I'll start by asking you what the core of the idea of "reading" means to you.

Fran: To me, reading means to be looking at words so as to understand what they mean.

Carver: This is almost exactly the same meaning I want to convey when I use the term "reading." Rauding is a special type of reading. I coined the term "rauding" to refer to those situations in which individuals are attending to words and are comprehending each consecutive thought they are presented.

"Reading" is often used in an extremely general way. For example, one past president of the International Reading Association, Donald L. Cleland, defined reading this way: "Reading is the cognitive process of perceiving and ordering your environment." To regard the word "reading" in this global way means that it includes what people do when they play chess or what a football coach does during a game. Such broad definitions for reading suit some purposes well, such as broadening the membership in a "reading" organization to include football coaches, but it is not very helpful for advancing knowledge about what happens most of the time when people interact with words.

I think I'll be able to communicate with you better if I elaborate further upon the concept of rauding. What I will be trying to do as we talk is draw a circle around those activities that I want to call "rauding." I will try to show you what rauding includes and what it does not include. By analogy, I will be trying to show you what part of air is properly called oxygen. Keep in mind, however, that I will not be trying to describe something new; "rauding" is something with which everyone is already familiar. I will be describing this familiar entity more precisely and then later developing laws that explain the facts associated with it.

Let me begin by saying that rauding would be involved in all those reading situations in which a person is attending to words in the form of meaningfully connected sentences (such as paragraphs in a reading passage) and is understanding or comprehending each consecutive thought as it is presented. Notice that I said "all those situations in which a person is attending to words in the form of meaningfully connected sentences." This means that, above all, I want you to understand that rauding may also be involved when words are presented orally. Rauding is not only an idea that applies to people looking at visually presented material, but it also applies to people listening to auditorily presented material. You probably remember from the original theory article that the word "rauding" was derived from a combination of the two words, "reading" and "auding." Notice that I pronounce "rauding" so it rhymes with "auding." "Auding" is considered as a parallel term to reading; auding means to listen to orally presented words, letters, or other language symbols to gain information or knowledge. So, the concept of rauding includes auding situations; don't make the mistake of thinking that rauding is restricted to reading situations. Although I am primarily interested in rauding as it occurs during reading, you should never forget that rauding occurs just as frequently, if not *more* frequently, during auding.

You should also make sure you understand the linear or sequential aspect of rauding. Rauding only occurs in those situations in which the person is understanding each consecutive thought that is presented. One of my purposes in developing this concept of rauding was to focus on the commonality between the processes that go on when listening to radio or television and when reading a book, magazine, or newspaper. Another of my purposes is to focus on a more fundamental component of reading.

Fran: I now understand how you want rauding to encompass certain commonalities between reading and auding. I'm not sure I understand how this fits in with your idea that rauding is a "more fundamental component of reading."

Carver: Rauding is a subset of reading, a fundamental and highly important part of all those activities that are called "reading." Let me elaborate again and then give you some examples. The idea of rauding was developed to get at a fundamental aspect of the communication of thoughts. When an author writes the sentences in a paragraph, or a set of paragraphs, the author is trying to express his or her thoughts in a way that the expected audience, the likely readers or auders, will understand them. Most written and spoken material is designed by its originator, the author, to be understood by a certain type of person, and most of the people who eventually attempt to understand this material are just the type of people the author was expecting. Thus, it is no accident that most of the time when a person is attending to written words or attending to spoken words that person is then very likely to be understanding each consecutive thought of the author's that is presented. In fact, if the person does not understand each consecutive thought, then it is highly likely that the individual will terminate the activity. Of course, there are important exceptions. Students are quite often given material that they do not understand, either in textbooks or in lectures, and not all of them terminate the attempt to understand just because they are not understanding each consecutively presented thought. This type of study activity engaged in by students is frequently called reading, yet it often has characteristics that are quite different from ordinary reading.

Typical reading is characterized by the understanding of each consecutive thought presented in the material; students "reading" textbooks, however, are more often *not* understanding each consecutive thought. Students are more likely to have to engage in auxiliary activities such as rereading sentences, previewing the entire book or chapter before beginning to read, taking notes on the material, underlining important points in the book, or memorizing certain parts.

As a student, Fran, what is the primary use you find for reading?

Fran: I read mostly when I study.

Carver: Tell me how you use "reading" in "studying."

Fran: I look at a passage in a textbook, and I try to understand it. If I can, I might make a note about it and go on.

Carver: If you can't?

Fran: Then I go back, sentence by sentence or word by word, and try to figure it out. I try to read it again. When I can read it straight through and understand it, I probably will make a note and go on.

Carver: You are talking about two different processes. I hope you see that.

Fran: I'm not sure.

Carver: You read and understand; that's one kind of reading you do. You read and figure it out, that's another. I'm saying we should not call these things by the same name. I want to call it "studying" when you say you are "reading and figuring it out" and I want to call it "rauding" when you say you are "reading and understanding."

Fran: Then, in a way, you could say that one of the purposes of studying is to be able to raud.

Carver: Yes. I see you rauding when you can and then switching to studying when you can't. It seems important to me to make sure that the type of typical reading activity that sometimes occurs during what you call "studying" is easily isolated if desired. One reason for developing the concept of rauding was to prevent the processes associated with the understanding of each consecutively presented thought from getting inextricably mixed up with the different process associated with studying. Thus, typical reading will be called rauding so that it can be isolated from what you call studying.

Fran: Since typical reading seems to mean the same thing to you as rauding, why don't you just delete "rauding" and use the much simpler terminology, "typical reading."

Carver: Aha, you have momentarily forgotten that rauding also encompasses a typical activity that occurs during auding, so this would not be an acceptable suggestion.

Fran: You are right this time, but I should warn you that I will be doing my best to find reasons why the concept of rauding is not necessary. I am generally against the development of technical terminology unless it is absolutely necessary.

Carver: I applaud your skeptical attitude. It is exactly the stance I would take if I were on the other side of the fence. If I could not perceive any advantage to someone else's new words, ideas, or theory, then I would be very hesitant to even learn about the theory, let alone accept it.

Fran: Your last comment has made me wonder if I have any needs that rauding theory could help me with.

Carver: As I explain rauding theory, I will relate to you the needs that I see being fulfilled by it. Then, you will have to judge for yourself whether rauding theory helps you.

In the reading literature, you will find people talking about "reading efficiency" and "percent comprehension," yet I found it impossible to make these terms operational. Percent comprehension could not mean something as simple as the percent of test questions answered correctly because test questions can be made easy or difficult. Furthermore, how could you measure whether a person was becoming more efficient as a reader if there was not some agreed-upon technique for measuring efficiency? We will get to my suggested solutions to these problems later. I think you can see, however, that if we don't tie down precisely what type of reading we wish to investigate — rauding, or studying, or skimming, or scanning, or memorizing — then it will be next to impossible to tie down what we mean by percent comprehension or efficient reading. But I'm straying again from your main question, what is rauding?

Fran: Let me try to put in my own words what I think you have told me so far. You want to isolate a certain part of all the activities that other people typically refer to as reading. Other people may use the term "reading" to refer to a host of activities that involve looking at words, but you want to focus upon just a portion of these activities and call them rauding.

Carver: That is true, but when you say it that way it sounds as though I am making a distinction that is drab or unimportant. I will use the word "reading" as a very general term that refers to all those situations in which individuals are looking at words, letters, or other language symbols to gain information, or knowledge. I am using the term *rauding* to refer to typical *reading* because I think there needs to be another conceptual term that is on approximately the same level as *scanning, skimming, studying,* and *memorizing.**

Fran: Don't most people in reading research and reading instruction already make these conceptual distinctions when they are called for?

Carver: Sometimes, but not nearly often enough, and the lack of a specific term such as "rauding" impedes such distinctions being made. There is a lot of research done under the rubric of "reading" that is really "studying" or "memorizing." The facts or laws that are discovered in this research will not generalize to typical reading — will not generalize to rauding. Furthermore, I think a lot of researchers are familiar with skimming, either through their own personal experience or by reading about the feats of speed readers, and they incorrectly make inferences from these activities to typical reading. They observe a speed reading performance and then make a generalization about reading, which may apply to skimming but does not apply to rauding. At the moment, I am simply saying that I think typical reading is qualitatively different enough from other types of reading to deserve its own category and distinctive label, namely

---

* A List of Rauding Theory Definitions is included in the Appendices. These words will be italicized the first time they appear in the text.

"rauding." Furthermore, I think it is not enough simply to call it typical reading since it appears to have so much in common with what goes on when people typically listen to orally presented thoughts. As I am talking to you I am making the assumption that you are rauding: that you are understanding each consecutive *thought* as I say it. From my standpoint, what is going on as you listen to what I say is almost the same as what would happen if my thoughts were typed up and presented to you for understanding in a visual mode or printed mode. Of course, the two processes start out differently in that the stimuli are quite different. If you were blind, you could auditorily *raud* but not visually raud, and if you were deaf, you could visually raud but not auditorily raud. Once the environmental stimuli in the form of words are perceived, however, the remainder of the activity has so much in common from one mode to the other that it seems convenient and helpful to refer to these two activities collectively as rauding.

It is my contention that most of the time that people are listening to orally presented language they are doing what I call rauding; they are rauding because they are *comprehending* each consecutive thought with which they are being presented. Stating the same thing another way, I would say that people are rauding 90 percent of the time they are *auding*. Furthermore, it is my contention that people are rauding 90 percent of the time they are reading. If at this moment we were able to take a thirty-second sample of the activities of all the 230 million people in the United States, just a fraction would be reading. Of all those people who were reading, I would hypothesize that the relative frequencies of those types of reading would be as follows: scanning, 1 percent; skimming, 1 percent; rauding, 90 percent; studying, 7 percent; memorizing, 1 percent.

I believe rauding is the most frequent thing that happens while people read. Rauding should not be confused with these other activities, which are qualitatively different. Before I continue, let me ask you what you think about my hypothesized percents.

Fran: I don't think I would agree that what you want to call "rauding" is quite that frequent or that studying and skimming are that infrequent. I would leave scanning and memorizing at 1 percent, or even lower, but I would increase skimming and studying to 3 percent and 15 percent respectively. That would reduce rauding to 80 percent.

Carver: We are not in very much disagreement. Yet, my opinion is that you are unduly influenced by your own experiences, which are heavily weighted by the schooling environment and are not representative of reading in general. In my original presentation of rauding theory, I referenced a researcher who found that only about 1 percent of his sample reported having any difficulty with any of the material that they had read recently. Thus, I interpreted his data as indicating that almost all reading involves the understanding of consecutive thoughts, which I call rauding, and that studying is an important activity but that it is confined to a small part of the population.

I do not want to give the impression that theory, research, and practice involving scanning, skimming, studying, or memorizing are not extremely important. Rather, I am not favorably impressed by the amount of theory, research, and practice devoted to rauding, considering that it accounts for 80 to 90 percent of all the reading that occurs.

Fran: When you said theory, research, and *practice* what did you mean by practice?

Carver: I mean to include all practical applications of knowledge that involve reading, such as the instruction teachers give to students who are learning to read. I believe that much of what is taught in schools is conducive to rauding, but I think we might be able to produce more and better rauders if practitioners, researchers, and theorists would agree that the primary goal that we are striving to accomplish is to produce better rauders.

Fran: I'm not sure I understand the point you are trying to make here.

Carver: When I see top-notch researchers studying what happens to eye movements as a person is attempting to memorize an isolated sentence, I wonder what relevance this has for rauding. When I see top-notch theorists speculating about how the hierarchical structure of passages affects recall after a student has studied the passage, I wonder what relevance this has for rauding. Don't get me wrong, I am not saying there *is* no relevance to rauding. There *may* be relevance. Furthermore, I do think these things are important in their own right. It bothers me a great deal, however, when I see researchers and theorists fail to make explicit discriminations among memorizing, studying, or skimming when they interpret the results of their "reading" research. Similarly, I see reading practitioners trying to help students with their reading problems by teaching them skimming skills and studying skills, and then they seemingly expect this instruction to help them raud better. This might happen, but I am skeptical, especially when the student is not a good rauder and the instruction doesn't acknowledge the unique characteristics of rauding through its training practices. I'm saying that it is plain that we won't get much further in reading research and reading practice unless we acknowledge by our actions that there are qualitatively different types of reading.

Well, as you have probably discerned, my zeal is getting the best of me. I should be showing you how rauding theory has helped me explain why certain things happen in reading instead of giving you an emotionally charged sales pitch to buy these ideas. Let's get back to your original question again. I hope that you have a good idea now of the kinds of things that may be properly referred to as rauding.

Fran: I have a much better idea than I had before. However, I'm not sure I would know how to differentiate between skimming and rauding, and there are probably occasions where I would be hard pressed to be able to discriminate between studying and rauding.

Carver: In a research study, it is relatively easy to infer whether a student is skimming, rauding, or memorizing from the conditions of the experiment — the so-called "demand characteristics." If the experimenter "demands" that the subject simply get a general idea of what is in a prose passage by (a) instructing the subject to read quickly for main ideas, (b) providing general or gist type of questions after reading, and (c) allowing little time for reading, then it seems reasonable to categorize this study as a skimming study instead of a rauding study. This means that it is questionable whether the subjects will raud, and therefore it is questionable whether the results of this research will generalize to rauding situations. To generalize the results of a reading experiment to rauding, it is important that the experimenter set up conditions that are conducive to rauding. For example, the experimenter could (a) instruct the subject to read normally, naturally, typically, or comfortably; (b) provide passages that can be rauded; (c) provide questions after reading that focus upon whether the complete thoughts contained in the sentences of passages were understood; and (d) provide time limits and instructions that are conducive to rauding. These experimental situations are likely to produce rauding. On the other hand, if the experimenter (a) instructs the subjects to memorize the words, (b) requires the subject to give a verbatim recall of the words, and (c) allows a great deal of time for the memorization to occur, then it seems reasonable to categorize this reading research as memorizing.

Fran: What you have just described seems okay for inferring whether subjects in a study are skimming or rauding or memorizing. Is there anything I could observe about a person who was reading that would allow me to decide whether the person was rauding or not?

Carver: If the person was a college student, for example, and was covering the words between 200 and 400 words per minute, (wpm) I would say that rauding was probably occurring. Below about 150 wpm, I would begin to wonder if this college student was memorizing, and above about 450 wpm, I would begin to wonder if skimming was occurring.

Fran: Wait a minute! How do you know that persons who present to themselves the thoughts in a passage at a rate of 1,000 wpm are not understanding each consecutive thought and are therefore rauding not skimming?

Carver: An excellent question. I would not know for sure without additional information about whether the thoughts were comprehended.

Fran: You mean that if you tested a person who read a passage at 1,000 wpm and found that the person had comprehended each thought, then you would say that the person had rauded the passage at a rate of 1,000 wpm?

Carver: Hmmmm . . . That is an extremely difficult question to answer. Before I proceed I must also say that it is an important question because it touches some of the fundamental problems inherent in doing research and inherent in generalizing from research.

Now, let me go on with your question. The answer is no, I would not conclude that the person was rauding at 1,000 wpm without some evidence that the person had not rauded the same material on a previous occasion. The person may have been skimming and then answering the questions on the basis of what was remembered from a prior rauding of the material.

Fran: Aren't you defining rauding as what happens between 150 and 450 wpm?

Carver: Well, rate of reading has been a key variable in reading research, but, the answer to this question is an emphatic no. However, I can see that I probably will not be able to convince you otherwise without getting much deeper into rauding theory. So if you don't mind, let me postpone any further attempt to answer this question until after I have explained a great deal more about the theory.

Chapter 2

WHAT IS THE RAUDING PROCESS?

Fran: You have been explaining to me what "rauding" is, but in your original presentation you also talked about the "rauding process." Would you explain to me what the *rauding process* is and how it relates to rauding?

Carver? Yes, that *is* an important distinction to clear up. At the beginning of our dialogue, I argued that there were important qualitative differences among scanning, skimming, rauding, studying, and memorizing. To better explain to you what the rauding process is, I need to expand these ideas. I am going to describe specific processes, which I will call scanning, skimming, rauding, studying, and memorizing. I'm going to write on the chalkboard a description of each of these processes associated with reading. I'd like for you to spend some time studying the description of each *process*.

A Scanning Process

Example Purpose: To find out if a particular item of information exists in a reading passage.

Description of this Scanning Process:

Step 1. Look in the vicinity of the first word in the passage.

Step 2. If the target information is perceived, then stop and record the find in some manner, e.g. make a mental note.

Step 3. If the target information is not perceived, then move the fixation point far enough away so that there is little or no overlap with first fixation but not so far that relevant information is skipped or not perceived.

Step 4. Repeat Steps 2 and 3 until end of passage is reached.

Example of Usage: To find out whether a passage contains information relevent to a specific topic by scanning words, headings, names, dates, etc. to see if any of this information can be used to answer a stated or implied question.

17

A Skimming Process

Example Purpose: To get an overview of a passage or to get the gist of a passage. To ascertain what the passage is about or what general information is included in the passage.

Description of this Skimming Process:

Step 1. *Look in the vicinity of the first sentence or the first part of the passage.*

Step 2. *Perceive a word or a small set of words and quickly make an inference about their meaning in connection with the goal of formulating an overview of the passage.*

Step 3. *Skip to the next line, or the next sentence, or the next paragraph, or the next page and repeat Step 2.*

Step 4. *Continue this sampling and inferring until end of passage is reached.*

Example Usage:

1. *To make sure that no information is missed that is of direct relevance to one's own information-seeking goals. When an inference is made that a sentence or a group of words contains highly important thoughts, then this skimming process may be stopped and the rauding process may be started.*

2. *To make sure one has at least a minimal amount of knowledge about a particular journal article, magazine article, court case brief, case history, etc.*

3. *To be a "jack of all trades; master of none" in the sense of knowing a little about a lot instead of knowing a lot about a little.*

The Rauding Process

Example Purpose: To understand the thoughts that the author of a passage intended to communicate.

Description of the Rauding Process (during reading but not auding):

Step 1. *Look in the vicinity of the first word in the passage and try to determine the meaning of that word as intended by the author.*

Step 2. *Try to determine the meaning of the second word in the same manner as the first, but move the fixation point, if necessary, to perceive the second word.*

Step 3. *Repeat Steps 1 and 2, always moving the fixation point just far enough to keep adding new words while attempting to formulate the thought represented by the words when the author wrote the sentence.*

Step 4. Continue with Steps 1 to 3 until the end of the sentence is reached and the thought (or thoughts) as intended by the author is either understood or not.

Step 5. Begin looking in the vicinity of the first word in the second sentence and repeat Steps 1-4.

Step 6. Continue Steps 1-4 until all of the sentences in the passage have been covered.

Example Uses:

1. To communicate with another individual; to understand the thoughts that another individual has expressed.

2. To profit from or be entertained by the experiences of another individual by comprehending that individual's thoughts.

A Studying Process

Example Purpose: To try to understand information in a passage that is relatively difficult.

Description of this Studying Process:

Step 1. Try to figure out the intended meaning of the words by hypothesizing about their meaning.

Step 2. Look at the words and take the time to check whether the hypothesis is supported or not.

Step 3. Repeat Steps 1 and 2 for each succeeding set of words and execute any of a number of problem-solving strategies when hypotheses are not confirmed.

Example Use: To try to educate oneself by making it possible to raud a passage that previously could not be rauded.

A Memorizing Process

Example Purpose: To increase the probability that the thoughts in a passage can be recalled on a subsequent occasion.

Description of this Memorizing Process:

Step 1. Look at the words in the passage in some manner that holds promise for remembering the thoughts later.

Step 2. Remove the passage from view and attempt to reconstruct the words or the thoughts.

Step 3. Check product against passage.

Step 4. When Step 3 fails, keep repeating Steps 1-3 until there is success.

Example Uses:

1. To be able to recall the ideas and information contained in a textbook so as to be able to do well on a subsequent examination.

2. To satisfy the requirements of a memory researcher, e.g. taking part in certain "prose learning" experiments.

Fran: I've tried to raud what you have put on the chalkboard. I have a number of questions. First, it seems to me that scanning is not necessarily serial as you seem to describe it. When I scan a phone book for a friend's number, I will skip to the page the number is on and then I usually only have to scan a few numbers to find the one I want.

Carver: Let me interrupt you before you go too far on this subject. I have presented these five detailed processes in the context of a *passage* because this is where rauding theory is most appropriate. Second, the *scanning process* that I have described is only one of several possible processes that might be classified as scanning. I am describing these particular nonrauding processes primarily to give you something with which to contrast rauding. Rauding theory does not purport to be a theory about scanning, skimming, studying, or memorizing processes. However, to understand the theory, it is first helpful to describe in some detail what it does not cover, and this in turn involves a certain amount of theorizing about scanning, skimming, studying, and memorizing. So that you can understand what the rauding process is, I find it necessary to compare and contrast it with these highly similar but qualitatively different things. These particular descriptions of scanning, skimming, studying, and memorizing processes no doubt can be improved and extended by theorists and researchers who are primarily interested in each particular activity.

I'm trying to say that I'd prefer that you not question me too much about the details of my description of these other processes unless your questioning has a direct consequence for understanding the rauding process or rauding.

Fran: Okay. I'll adhere to that rule, Professor! I'm still a little uncertain about what the difference is between "rauding" and the "rauding process."

Carver: I'm not surprised! This has been one of my major problems in communicating the theory to others. Let me review.

Rauding is the understanding, or comprehending, of each successive thought as the thoughts are being presented. This definition of rauding covers an activity that frequently occurs in the United States, as well as other countries in the world. Most of the time that people are said to be reading, they will be rauding. Rauding theory will focus upon rauding as it occurs during reading. However, rauding also occurs most of the time that you can observe that a person is listening to another person talk. This definition of rauding is a product definition in that it refers to situations where each thought is being understood as it is being presented. For example, if you observed an individual was not understanding each thought as the speaker presented it, then this would not be called rauding. Perhaps you will recall that in my original presentation of the theory I relaxed this definition somewhat. In connection with passages, I said that rauding involved the understanding of "most" of the thoughts as they were encountered, and I further gave an operational rule of thumb for deciding what "most" was. I said that if at least 75 percent of the thoughts being presented in a passage were being understood then this would be called rauding. I'd like to get back to this, later. For now, you should understand that rauding involves reading and auding situations that have a certain product or outcome.

The rauding process was outlined in the six steps in Drawing 3 that I put on the chalkboard. The main difference between the rauding process and rauding is that a person may be *operating* or carrying out the steps of the rauding process — attempting to comprehend thoughts as they are being presented — but still not be successful in this effort. Thus, the rauding process may be occurring, or operating, but the individual not be rauding. An alternative way of describing this situation might be to say that the individual may be unsuccessful in his/her attempt to raud. Operation of the rauding process is a necessary but not sufficient condition for rauding to occur. *Operation of the rauding process is necessary for rauding to occur, but the operation of the rauding process is not sufficient to produce rauding.*

Fran: I can understand that a person might be using a communication process without communicating. It seems to me that this is similar to what you are saying when you say that a person can be executing the rauding process without rauding.

Carver: That's right.

Fran: I can also see that it could be considered as impossible to communicate without using a communication process. So, I can understand why you say that execution of the rauding process is necessary for rauding to occur.

Carver: Right again. However, I think I should warn you about some possible inconsistencies. As is the case with many words, we learn to use them as effortlessly as possible so that you might hear me talking to someone about his/her rauding research project and I might say, "You mean to tell me that you found that your subjects were rauding less than 25 percent of the thoughts in your study?" This would not be a perfectly proper way of using the term rauding since it is supposed to be used only to designate situations where most (more than 75%), if not all, of the thoughts are being understood. Technically, I should have said, "You mean to tell me that your test data indicated that your subjects were only comprehending 25 percent of the thoughts while they were operating the rauding process?" However, "operating the rauding process" gets to be an unnecessary mouthful when you are talking to someone who knows from the context exactly what you are talking about.

Fran: I think I can cope with those minor inconsistencies.

Carver: Good. The existence of rauding is something that I have assumed that you would give me without argument. I am hesitant to bring it up, but you could disagree that rauding exists. I hope you do not need to be convinced that there are many situations or events that occur each day in this world where people are comprehending successive thoughts as they read them. We might argue about the importance of rauding, the frequency of rauding, the processes that occur during rauding, or the definition of rauding. But if we cannot agree that this phenomenon that I have called "rauding" exists, then we are not communicating at a fundamental level, and there is no need to continue until we get that part settled. In short, I hope you understand that the existence of rauding is a fundamental assumption of rauding theory.

Fran: I raud you loud and clear. I do agree that the phenomenon you want to refer to by use of the word "rauding" exists. I am not totally convinced that this is the best word to use to name that phenomenon, but I am willing to concede and use your word for the time being. Maybe later I'll be more organized in my own thoughts and I may find some good reason for not using the term rauding.

Carver: Fair enough! We now agree that rauding exists. The rauding process is simply the activities or steps that operate making rauding possible. It seems important to study *the* rauding process. However, it does *not* seem important to study *the* reading process. This is because there is no single process associated with reading. Reading has many different and distinct processes associated with it. It is my contention that we will not make much progress in our attempts to expand knowledge about reading as long as we continue to talk about *the* reading process. There was not much progress in attempts to expand knowledge about air as long as it was unrecognized that air contained more fundamental elements with distinctly different properties. Similarly, reading contains more fundamental elements with distinctly different properties. Just as oxygen is an important component of air and deserves special attention, I think that the rauding process is an important component of reading and deserves special attention. It seems to me that *the* reading process is usually intended to refer to *the* rauding process, but too often it is impossible to be sure that this is the case. I keep mentioning studying, skimming, etc., only to help you see what activities are in bounds and what activities are out of bounds for circumscribing what is considered to be rauding and not rauding.

Fran: I understand your purpose but I'm not sure but what you are confusing me. For example, what you call *studying process* cannot be the only thing that occurs when people are said to be "studying." Do you consider this being picky?

Carver: No. I realize that each of the nonrauding processes that I have described is just one of many possible activities that might carry exactly the same name. For example, I use the word "studying" to describe a collection of activities. Any time a person uses a receptive activity such as a scanning process, a *skimming process,* a rauding process, a studying process, or a *memoriz-*

ing process as part of a strategy for increasing one's understanding or future recall of information then this would be called "studying." Also included in this list of activities called studying would be such productive activities as note taking, underlining, reciting, and outlining. Thus, studying is a generic term that may involve a host of different processes and activities. I have defined one specific process that can reasonably be called a studying process. Similarly, I have defined one specific process that can reasonably be called a skimming process. Again, each of the four nonrauding processes have been defined primarily so that they can be contrasted with the rauding process.

You would think that no one would do research that involved a person using a scanning process and then interpret the results as if they applied equally well for the rauding process. Yet, there exists a great deal of such scanning research that has been conducted under the rubric of "reading," and when the results are interpreted, generalizations will often be made about reading in general without stopping to question whether the results apply to situations where the rauding process is used. The scanning process and the rauding process both relate to reading but are processes that have little more in common other than they both involve looking at words — they have no more in common than do oxygen and nitrogen, which both happen to be gases that exist together in air.

At the other end of the spectrum is memorizing. Again, you would think that no one would have the audacity to do research where the subject's task was to provide verbatim recall of all the words in sentences and then suggest without question that the results applied to the rauding process. Yet, this is the way that I see a great deal of "reading" research. It is relatively easy to infer qualitative differences between the rauding process and those other two processes, scanning and memorizing, which occupy the poles of the spectrum.

Fran: Let me interrupt a moment. Why do you refer to the "poles of the spectrum"?

Carver: I guess I neglected to mention that the five reading processes that I have described in detail did not just happen to be presented in the order I gave them to you. The order is in an ascending order of time required to gain the desired ends of reading. For example, if I had a 2,000-word prose passage and I asked you to perform a scanning task, I would expect you to finish that task much more quickly than if I asked you to memorize the passage. Thus, scanning and memorizing represent the two extremes of the spectrum with respect to time, or rate. You should operate this scanning process on a passage faster than you would this skimming process. You should operate this skimming process on a passage faster than the rauding process. You should operate the rauding process faster than you would this studying process. And, you should operate this studying process faster than you would this memorizing process.

Don't make the mistake, however, of assuming that these activities are primarily just quantitatively different. The reason they are quantitatively different is that they are qualitatively different processes. The cumulative time required to finish a passage varies with each of the five processes because each process involves steps that require different amounts of time even though each process may involve certain activities that require equal amounts of time, such as perceiving a word during a fixation.

Fran: You have discussed how the rauding process relates to a scanning process, a studying process, and a memorizing process. I assume you will do the same for the skimming process you outlined.

Carver: Okay. During the operation of this skimming process, the individual is *not* trying to understand each consecutive thought that the author intended to communicate. In thought communication situations, senders try to adjust the quantity and quality of the information so that receivers are likely to be neither overwhelmed by too much nor bored by too little. The preparer (sender) of a prose passage is striving to communicate with those who attempt to raud the passage (receiver). So, the sender tries not to make the sentences too long or too short, for example. Sentence length has little or no effect upon the skimming process. The nature of the sentences has very little direct influence upon these skimming activities because sentences are irrelevant units when skimming. On the other hand, the length of sentences does have an impact upon what happens during the rauding process. If you construct a passage that contains a sentence eighty words long, most people will not be able to comprehend it, so a shift will probably be made to a studying process. The nature of the sentence resulted in a failure to successfully operate the rauding process, so the rauding process was interrupted. Since the comprehension of the thought or thoughts contained in an eighty-word sentence is not involved in the skimming process, such a sentence has little or no effect upon the skimming process. Skimming processes usually involve a sampling of information and then the making of inferences about the population of information based upon hypotheses about that population. Do you think you understand the qualitative difference between the skimming process and rauding process?

Fran: Yes, mostly, but I'm not sure I have one thing straight. Isn't it possible for a person to skim an article using a skimming process and still understand all of the thoughts the author intended to communicate, in which case we would have to say that rauding occurred as a result of the operation of the skimming process?

Carver: I remember that you asked that question earlier and I postponed the answer at that time. Now, I'll try to handle it. This question gets at whether we can in fact make empirical distinctions between theoretically different phenomena. You are asking, using the previous analogy, is it possible to isolate oxygen from air and then find that it has the properties of hydrogen? Obviously, if we do, something is drastically wrong. Likewise, we have a major problem if we find people who seemingly are executing a skimming process yet show evidence that they comprehended each sentence in the passage. The problem is that I have described this skimming process in such a way that it was supposed to be more effective by skipping words and not attempting to comprehend each complete thought represented by a sentence. So, if each sentence is being comprehended, this is inconsistent with the purported nature of the skimming process. One factor that could produce this type of incongruity would be a major theoretical deficiency. In which case, the next decision would be whether to throw the theory out or to start modifying it drastically. Another factor that could produce this result could be a major empirical deficiency. For example, it is possible that the individual had previously memorized the passage, quickly skipped over the sentences when observed, and was subsequently able to show great comprehension of the sentences because they had already been memorized. If rauding theory is seriously considered by interested researchers, then I hope that it is subjected to empirical test in situations where it is unreasonable to assume that the skimmer has previously memorized, studied, or rauded the experimental passages. Then, we will find out if it is possible or impossible for each consecutive thought in a passage to be comprehended as a result of the operation of a skimming process.

Fran: When a theory is presented, isn't there an automatic invitation to researchers to test the theory to determine its weaknesses?

Carver: Yes, I'm just trying to head off research being conducted that seemingly refutes rauding theory but in fact does not have the necessary experimental controls over important variables.

In an experiment, one of the best ways to get an idea about whether it is likely that the rauding process was actually operating is to look at the rate at which the subject read the experimental materials. There are occurrences in the research literature where college students chose to read sentences at rates around 100 words per minute, yet the investigator would seem to interpret the results as if they were automatically relevant to the rauding process. Of course, the terminology "rauding process" would not be used, but the idea was implied just the same by the use of the term "reading" or "reading process." Since the average college student rauds at about 300 words per minute, it is possible, but very improbable, that the rauding process occurs when college students take part in an experiment and choose to read at 100 words per minute. Thus, on this type of evidence alone, it seems more reasonable to infer that the students were operating a studying process or maybe even a memorizing process.

Fran: I would like to see if I can summarize the difference between rauding and the rauding process. The rauding process involves the perception of each consecutive word in a passage, and then each perceived word is used by the individual to formulate each consecutive thought that the author intended to communicate when the author wrote the sentences. If the purpose of this process is fulfilled, then the individual is said to be rauding. Now, I'm not sure if you want rauding theory to apply only to rauding situations or if you want it to apply only to those situations in which the rauding process is involved?

Carver: That question is a good one because it allows the domain of rauding theory to be neatly delineated. The theory is appropriate for all situations involving the rauding process. This means that it will not only cover rauding situations but also those nonrauding situations which involve the unsuccessful operation of the rauding process. Still, a primary goal of the theory is to be able to explain experimentally verifiable facts about rauding. I will use the terminology "rauding theory" to refer to the definitions, assumptions, principles, laws, hypotheses, and equations that deal with rauding and the rauding process.

Fran: So, you are saying that if there are rational grounds for inferring that the rauding process is not operating in a certain situation then it is not appropriate to use rauding theory to explain or predict in that situation. You are saying that research results which come from situations wherein it is not reasonable to infer that the rauding process was operating should not be used to make inferences about rauding.

Carver: Correct.

Fran: I have a much better idea now of what you mean by rauding and the rauding process. I'm looking forward to getting deeper into the more theoretical aspects of rauding theory.

Chapter 3

WHAT IS THEORY?

Carver: I hope I won't disappoint you too much, but I don't think I can explain the details of rauding theory to you without digressing again to make sure you understand "theory." What does theory mean to you?

Fran: A theory is an explanation of why things are the way they are. There may be different or competing theories to explain the same things. Research helps to determine which one is best.

Carver: Not bad! One of the best ways to evaluate the worth of a theory is in terms of its predictions. Some theories are extremely well proven, or supported. They are not tenuous at all because the predictions made from the theory have turned out to be correct or accurate. Einstein's special theory of relativity is a modern example of a theory that seems to enjoy a great deal of support in terms of real world predictions turning out correctly. It is important to understand that a theory may be a theory whether it is tenuous or not, whether it is proven or not, whether it has empirical support or not.

I liked the part of your definition about a theory being a way of explaining things. Scientific theories tend to be complicated explanations in the sense that they cannot, ordinarily, be articulated in a single sentence. A theory involves interconnecting various concepts, ideas, or variables.

Let me expand on theory because you need to understand what I am trying to accomplish with rauding theory. It will be impossible for you to appreciate whatever merits it might have if you don't have a relatively firm background in scientific theory.

The two main goals of science generally are considered to be explanation and prediction. "Explanation" is more associated with the concepts and ideas created by humans and articulated by language, while "prediction" is more associated with happenings, events, or processes of the world that can be observed. A

29

theory is developed by humans to explain why certain observable things occur. Pasteur developed the theory that alcoholic fermentation occurred — an empirically observable event — because living organisms, microscopic in size, were eating yeasts and giving off alcohol and CO_2. The idea was that fermentation involved the life cycle of a living bug. This theory explained many known facts about fermentation, such as that warmer temperatures speed up things but hot temperatures stop the process completely. Before Pasteur, you might have asked the question "Why does milk spoil?" and gotten an answer such as, it spoils because there are certain chemical reactions that occur when yeast is added to certain solutions. After Pasteur, you get an answer such as, milk spoils because certain unwanted living micro-organisms have grown and multiplied. A theory explains why observed events occur, so a theory may be evaluated in terms of how well it accounts for these previously observed events. More importantly, however, a theory may be used to predict new events and can thus be evaluated in terms of how accurate the predictions are.

Fran: Therefore, if I understand you correctly, I ought to be able to evaluate rauding theory in terms of how well it explains existing data as well as how accurately it can predict things that may not have been of interest or suspected prior to the development of the theory.

Carver: Exactly. A theory should explain why certain facts existed prior to the theory, and it should be a tool to develop new facts.

Because a good theory can be used to predict future events accurately, humans can use good theories to manipulate and control events. For example, from Pasteur's theory it can be predicted that spoiling can be prevented by heating milk to a temperature where the unwanted microorganisms are killed and therefore cannot grow and produce spoilage. In the area of reading, if we can theorize well, it may be that certain predictions based upon the theory will allow us to facilitate growth in the reading ability of individuals. However, such successful practical applications are not necessary for a theory to be a good one. For a theory to be good, it must explain well what it purports to explain. Furthermore, the various deductions or predictions made from the theory must be shown to be accurate.

It is also reasonable and proper for critics to point out what a theory does *not explain*. This type of criticism helps to clarify the theory. However, it is not reasonable or proper to deprecate a theory because it does not explain something that it was not designed to explain.

Fran: In recent years there has been a great deal of discussion about reading models. How is a model different from a theory? Is rauding a model of reading?

Carver: That's a complicated question, and I'm afraid my answer will be of the same caliber. There are many ways of viewing models and theory, but I think it will be best if you first understand a model as an analogy. Many theories, especially the well-accepted ones, incorporate an analogy (model) borrowed from another area or theory. For example, Pasteur's theoretical ideas were articulated by using a farming, or agriculture model (analogy). Pasteur conceived fermentation as a growth situation that was analogous to growing crops on a farm. If you wanted the crops to grow faster you would add "manure." By analogy, this means that you would add a protein product to solutions that contain microorganisms that you wanted to grow.

Another example of a model (analogy) is the use of the flow of water as an analogy (model) for explaining the flow of heat. Thermodynamics borrowed the theoretical ideas that had already been developed for the flow of fluids and applied them to heat and found them to work well as a model — water flow was a successful analogy for heat flow.

In reading, the idea of a model as an analogy is less direct but still useful. A model in reading is a mechanism (an organization of ideas, such as farming) used as an analogy. However, a model in reading would not likely be an analogy as familiar or success-ful, as farming or water flow. Rather, the analogy is more likely to take the form of boxes with arrows connecting the boxes. Certain researchers have tried to conceive of processes involved in reading using boxes and arrows, and they hope that this conception will be analogous enough to the actual events so that they can explain and predict certain reading phenomena.

As I suggested before, analogies borrowed from other areas (models) have been an inherent part of many successful theories in science. All scientific theories have a verbal schema (called a model), which articulates the interrelationships among its logically related aspects. Some philosophers of science may define a theory in a way that necessarily includes a model, whether it is an analogy borrowed from another area or not. In the reading research literature, however, we find many models of the reading process, but we seldom find a more encompassing theory in which one of these models is embedded.

I may have told you more than you care to know about models; let me try to summarize. A model is best regarded as an analogy that helps articulate a theory, such as the farming model used in the theory of fermentation. In reading, the analogies often take the form of flow charts or diagrams with lines drawn between boxes. If the model (analogy) is not borrowed from a highly familiar area, it is likely to be difficult to understand, less likely to be accepted, and the implications of the model are less likely to be perceived and tested. Stated differently, a theory that is able to incorporate meaningfully a model that is familiar or readily understood is more likely to be seriously considered and tested.

When rauding theory was originally presented it was called a model by one of its critics, and I was very defensive about this. I was defensive because I had called this collection of ideas a "theory," and it was stinging to my ego for someone to suggest that I had made a mistake because the proper name for this set of ideas was "model," not "theory." After a great deal of study of the matter I have come to two conclusions. First, it would be a violation of "truth in labeling" laws to refer to these ideas as a "rauding model" instead of "rauding theory"; this collection of ideas is properly referred to as a theory, not a model. It is a collection of interrelationships among concepts that attempt to explain certain experimental facts. It is not simply an analogy. Second, if I could someday conceive of a familiar model (analogy) that fit well into rauding theory, then the theory would offer greater benefits to the field because of the political realities about familiar models that I mentioned earlier.

I've talked a lot without giving you a chance to speak.

Fran: That's okay. Are you finished with theory now?

Carver: Not quite! When I originally presented rauding theory, it was presented more from the standpoint of an empiricist than a rationalist. I'm going to try to help you understand the theory this time by reversing these two positions.

Fran: I assume you will first explain what you mean by empiricist and rationalist in this context, won't you?

Carver: It occurs to me that you might be interested in doing some outside rauding in the theory of science. I would highly recommend George Gale's recent book, *Theory of Science.*[1] It is designed for the beginning student; it is raudable, interesting, and presents the basic ideas needed for you to evaluate any theory, including rauding theory. More important, however, it provides a general context for understanding why we do research, why we theorize, what rewards we can expect from scientific efforts, and how we can evaluate the theory and research efforts of others. My previous references to Lavoisier and Pasteur were directly stimulated by Gale's treatment of these individuals and their contributions. I will continue to draw upon what he has written to help me explain various points.

Fran: I guess I would probably benefit from a richer background in the philosophy of science, so I will at least try to take a look at that book.

Carver: Fair enough. Back to empiricism versus rationalism. An empiricist is one who focuses upon observations and the generalizations that can be made from them. Empiricists generally eschew theory and the deductions that can be made from theory. The most illustrative modern example of an empiricist is B. F. Skinner, who is noted for one publication that contains only data, tables, and figures.

The rationalists represent the other extreme. Rationalistic scientists focus upon reason. They believe that it is possible to conceive how things really are in general and then deduce particular empirical occurrences. Data collection, or experiments, are only undertaken when needed to choose between alternative

---

1. George Gale, *Theory of Science: An Introduction to the History, Logic, and Philosophy of Science* (New York, McGraw-Hill, 1979).

deductions. The most famous modern example of the rationalist position is Albert Einstein.

When I wrote the original account of rauding theory, I wrote it more from an empiricist position. I stuck fairly close to the data and used the formal terms "generalizations" and "hypotheses." The generalizations were suggested by previously collected data and were so noted. The hypotheses were more tentative, but they too were usually tied very closely to existing data.

I am neither a pure empiricist nor a pure rationalist. My approach to scientific research is probably about halfway between these two extreme positions. This means that I think that progress in education and psychology will be optimal when there is a balance between theory/rationale and data/experiments. My own surmise is that in the recent past there has been too much of an accent upon empiricism, no doubt partly attributable to the monumental influence of B. F. Skinner. The more recent upswing of cognitive psychology indicates to me that there is a movement away from the extreme empiricist position.

Fran: I'm getting a little lost. What does this have to do with rauding theory?

Carver: I was trying to prepare you for my embracing more of a rationalist position as I explain rauding theory to you. Instead of focusing upon data and what can be generalized from them, I am going to focus upon what principles can be reasoned about rauding; I shall then derive laws from these principles, derive hypotheses from the laws, and finally present the data that seem to support the hypotheses. Rauding theory will not undergo any substantive change in that there will not be new or different relationships purported among the variables in the theory. However, this rationalistic presentation will be an alternative way of expressing and communicating the theory. I hope it will be easier for you to follow than the original presentation was for many people. Even if it is not easier, I hope that you will benefit from having two elaborations of the same thing.

My goal will not be simply for you to understand rauding theory. I also hope that you will learn to evaluate the theory as we go along. Remember, one way you can evaluate a theory is by how well it explains. This means how well it answers "why" questions. However, before it can answer "why" questions, there must be something to explain or ask "why" about. When I finish telling you about rauding theory, you should be able to evaluate it in terms of how well it explains previously known facts, such as empirical or experimental data. You should also be able to evaluate how well the predictions made from the theory (which was constructed to explain previously known facts) are able to predict accurately new facts. Translated, this last facet of the evaluation means that you should be able to evaluate the theory in terms of how well hypotheses derived from the laws of the theory are supported by data that were collected to test these hypotheses.

Fran: Again, I don't believe you're telling me much that is new, but I do appreciate the review. I am anxious to get on to rauding theory in particular. It might help me if you gave me a little historical information. How did rauding theory get started?

Chapter 4

HOW DID RAUDING THEORY GET STARTED?

Carver: I'm glad you asked that question about the origins of rauding theory because it gives me a good chance to show you how the theory was developed to explain a particular experimental result.

I was doing some research on the dilation of the pupil of the eye. I videotaped one eye of college students as they read four passages of equal length but which varied in difficulty from very easy to very difficult. Although the results of that research did not support my hypothesis that pupil dilation is a measure of information processing, there was a serendipitous side effect. I was looking at the measured rate at which these students read, and I noticed something peculiar. When I measured reading rate in the conventional manner — by counting the total number of words in a passage and dividing by the amount of time in minutes that the student took to read the passage — I found that reading rate in *words per minute (wpm)* declined as the difficulty of the passage increased. This part of my results was not peculiar; in fact I had expected it. There is an informally accepted law in reading that people, especially good readers such as college students, adjust their reading rate to match the difficulty of the material they are reading, speeding up for easier material and slowing down for more difficult material.

Since I was a novice in the area, I was surprised when I noticed that the four passages were only superficially equal in length. They were all approximately 100 words long. Yet, when the four passages were typed on a page, the easier passages were in fact shorter on the page than the more difficult passages. Of course, as you well know, what I had discovered is what most people in reading are quite familiar with: more difficult passages tend to have longer words, on the average, than easier passages, no matter how you decide to measure passage difficulty. When I discovered for myself this empirical law about reading material, I immediately decided that it was somehow not proper to compare reading rate across these four passages when they were not equal in physical length. I decided to develop a way to measure rate that controlled for word length. This means that I developed the idea of a *standard length word* that contained a constant number of letters.

When I measured rate in terms of standard length words per minute, I found something peculiar. Much to my amazement, the empirical support for the previously noted law had evaporated. No longer did the data support the generalization that reading rate decreases as the difficulty of the material increases. No longer did the data support the idea that people slow down when the material that they are reading becomes more difficult. In fact, the first three of my four passages were read at almost exactly the same rate in standard length words per minute. There *was* a drop in rate for the last passage, the most difficult one; nevertheless it was still shocking to see the equality of rate in "standard length words" per minute for the first three passages. These three passages varied considerably in difficulty, they were read at considerably different rates in words per minute (wpm), yet the rate in standard length words per minute was nearly identical.

Fran: Surely you did not conclude from this one study of yours that you had refuted the generally accepted empirical law that reading rate declines as the reading material increases in difficulty.

Carver: No, that wasn't what I was trying to do. But the seed was planted for trying to explain why I found equal reading rates when the passages were not equal in difficulty. The harder I looked, the less support I found for the empirical generalization that reading rate declines as difficulty of the material increases. In fact, the more I looked at the data that others had collected and published prior to my private discovery, the more convinced I became that my data were reliable. It appeared that there was a systematic reason behind this failure of the traditional reading laws to explain what constancy there was in reading rate.

Fran: So the data convinced you that there was something reliable about the results and that previous theory was not able to explain it. But what about the fact that the most difficult passage was read slower, as you told me earlier?

Carver: This is where rauding came in. I speculated that the constancy of rate for the three easiest passages was likely to involve rauding and the rauding process while the decrease in rate for the most difficult passage was less likely to involve rauding or the rauding process. So this is where rauding theory began, with the beginning of an explanation for why reading rate tended to be constant across a wide range of material difficulty, or passage difficulty. Rauding theory grew by leaps and bounds thereafter. I would read the research literature and be stimulated to develop the explanation in detail so that it was not inconsistent with other known facts. Then, I began to collect data. I may appear to have been stimulated primarily by an empiricist bent, but in fact I was more stimulated to test the hypotheses of rauding theory. Thus, the data had more of a rationalistic heritage.

Fran: What did you mean when you said your research "may appear to have been stimulated more by an empiricist bent"?

Carver: Later, much later, when I get around to showing you the data that support rauding theory, you will see that the rationale given for collecting the data often gives little or no attention to rauding theory. Sometimes, it is only when the results get discussed that it is mentioned that the data support rauding theory. If I had focused upon rauding theory when I reported this research, it might have appeared that the data meant very little outside of rauding theory. I think the data can stand alone as empirical or experimental fact even without rauding theory, so I wrote up the research without depending on the theory.

I am trying to prepare you for coping with a person (me) who is in the middle, between a rationalist and an empiricist. Sometimes I see definite advantages to presenting things from one perspective and sometimes from the other. To reiterate, the research data that I will show you later will be presented more from the perspective of an empiricist, even though the main purpose in collecting the data was rationalistic in the sense that the research was primarily designed to test rauding theory.

My presentation of rauding theory to you, which will begin in a few minutes, will be presented more from the perspective of a rationalist, even though the original presentation of the theory was more from the perspective of an empiricist.

Fran: Are you sure I have to understand all of this before I am able to understand rauding theory?

Carver: Well . . . I guess not! I suppose the main reason I am telling you this now is so that you will remember it later when you have certain insights if I sometimes appear to be inconsistent and switch back and forth from the two positions. Hopefully, you will realize that I switched positions knowingly, because the situations needed different approaches.

Fran: Could we get on to rauding theory itself?

Carver: By all means!

Chapter 5

WHAT ARE THE PRINCIPLES OF RAUDING THEORY?

Carver: I am going to present to you a description of the theoretical system. The presentation of this theoretical rationale will be organized around several principles. These principles will deal with more details about the rauding process. For example, I will tell you what purportedly influences the rate at which this process operates.

Earlier, when I talked about rauding and the rauding process, I was mainly putting labels on processes and things that were already familiar to you. Now, I am going to elaborate and become more theoretical. I am going to step out on a theoretical limb, so to speak, and describe many of the interconnections I think exist among eye movements, subvocalization, speed of mental functioning, rate of reading, accuracy of comprehension, etc. These ideas are distinctively theoretical because they may be used later to explain and predict certain experimental data.

Do you have any questions before I proceed with the theory?

Fran: No, I'm just glad we are finally ready to get into the things that are more theoretical. This was the part that was the most difficult for me to understand when I tried to raud your original presentation.

Carver: The rauding process operates with the goal of understanding each consecutive thought that the author wanted to communicate when the sentences in a passage were composed. The first principle relevant to the operation of the process is that each word is used by the individual as a building block to reconstruct the thoughts of the author. It is impossible, according to the theory, for the individual to form the thoughts the author intended to communicate by skipping over words. This does not mean that there must be a fixation point centering on one of the letters of each word. It is sometimes possible to perceive a word

40

in the periphery of the eye without fixating directly upon it.

Fran: Does this mean that it is possible to perceive three or four words or even an entire line with one fixation?

Carver: No, I don't mean that.

However, to explain better what I mean, I need to introduce another principle. While the rauding process is operating, each word is being internally articulated.

Fran: What exactly do you mean by internal articulation?

Carver: I mean that a word is registered or encoded in a way that is best described as follows: people say each word to themselves while they raud.

Fran: You mean that the person is subvocalizing each word.

Carver: Yes, but don't get the idea that the rauding process is simply the same as oral reading except it is done silently. There are at least three ways that oral reading may be different from internal articulation. Oral reading *may* be done with very little effort made to understand the thoughts represented by the words being pronounced. Also, oral reading may proceed more slowly than internal articulation because there is a need for taking the time to articulate the word out loud in a manner that is intelligible to other people. Finally, when oral reading is done where the person can easily raud the thoughts in the passage, the pronunciation of the words out loud may be distracting to the most efficient operation of the rauding process.

The theory is that an individual perceives each word, internally articulates it, and, while doing this, attempts to formulate the thoughts the author intended to communicate.

Fran: Do we raud with internal articulation when we listen to speech?

Carver: Yes. I discussed the research that supports my affirmative answer to this question in my original presentation of the theory.

Fran: Can you be a little more precise about a thought? Can a word be a thought? Can a phrase be a thought? Can a sentence or a passage be a thought?

Carver: The thoughts the author intended to communicate ordinarily cannot be represented by a word. Sometimes a phrase or a clause might constitute a thought. Rather than be precise with respect to exactly what constitutes a thought, I have another principle that should be helpful. It is that the communication of thoughts from the author to the individual is accomplished via the comprehension of the complete thoughts that the author wrote down in the form of sentences. The principle is as follows: it is impossible for an individual to complete the communication process that the author initiated when he/she wrote down the sentences without comprehending the complete thoughts represented by the sentences. Comprehending each consecutive sentence, then, is the major function of the rauding process because this is considered to be necessary for the individual to receive the thoughts the sender intended to transmit.

Fran: I asked you a question earlier about fixations and you promised to answer it later. Are you ready yet?

Carver: Yes, I am. The eye movements must proceed down a line in a manner that allows each word to be perceived, internally articulated, and checked for meaning in terms of making complete thoughts out of the sentences in the passage.

Eye movements also have a more complex relationship to the rauding process, which I want to discuss shortly. For now, let me say that rauding theory holds that it is impossible for the rauding process to operate when there is only one fixation per line or one fixation every three or four words. There must be time for determining (a) what word it is, (b) the meaning of the word in the context of the sentence, and (c) the contribution of the word to the author's thought in the context of the passage. Recognizing a word in a sentence takes a certain amount of time. Determining the meaning of a word in a sentence takes an additional amount of time. If the word must be used to formulate a thought in the context of a passage, this will take an additional amount of time. Given that each of these parts of the process associated with each word takes a certain amount of time, it is considered to be impossible for the process to operate successfully without a fixation that centers upon almost every word in a passage. Short words such as "a," "of," "or," etc. may be perceived in a fixation that centers upon an adjoining word, but these small function words are still internally articulated and checked for meaning. They are likely to require less processing time simply because they are shorter, not less important for formulating the complete thought in a sentence.

Fran: Let me see if I can summarize what I think I have learned. Rauding theory holds that a person operates the rauding process for the purpose of understanding the thoughts in a passage — individuals operate the rauding process so as to raud. During the process, the individual centers a fixation upon almost every word, says each consecutive word to himself/herself, and attempts to comprehend the complete thought represented by the words in a sentence.

Carver: Excellent. Let *me* summarize by listing the principles we have covered so far and give a keyboard name to each principle.

> *Principle 1:* Word-for-word. During the rauding process, each consecutive word in the sentences of a passage is perceived and used to try to formulate the thoughts the author intended to communicate.
>
> *Principle 2:* Subvocalization. Each consecutive word in a passage is internally articulated during the operation of the rauding process.
>
> *Principle 3:* Sentences. The attempt to comprehend the complete thought contained in each consecutive sentence of a passage is a primary function of the rauding process.
>
> *Principle 4:* Eye Fixations. An eye fixation is centered upon almost every word in a passage during the operation of the rauding process.

Before I go on any further, it is important that I clarify a couple of things. It may have appeared to you earlier that I was defining by description what the rauding process was. It is now my task to disentangle for you exactly what the reading process is, by definition, and what its attributes are, from the standpoint of theory. By definition, the rauding process is the process used by the individual to try to comprehend each thought as it is consecutively encountered or presented. The rauding process is the process used by an individual to try to comprehend each consecutive thought in a passage that the author intended to communicate whether the words used to express the thoughts have been presented auditorily or visually. The earlier description of the eye movements associated with the rauding process was not intended to be included as part of the definition of the rauding process. Instead, these theorized steps were given to describe the rauding process in a more concrete way and to contrast it with other rauding processes.

Rauding and the rauding process are both givens in the theory; it is an assumption of the theory that rauding and the rauding process exist. The four principles we just discussed make it possible to give a more complete description of what the rauding process is theorized to involve. These theoretical principles assert that when an individual operates the rauding process on a passage, the following activities are involved: perceiving and internally articulating each consecutive word in an attempt to comprehend each consecutive sentence and thereby understand all the thoughts. During reading, it is further theorized, in the form of Principle 4, that the rauding process also involves a fixation on almost every word in a passage.

Fran: I think I understand the differences among your definitions, assumptions, and theoretical principles.

Carver: Now that I have finished giving you a more elaborate theoretical description of the principles concerning the nature of the rauding process, I would like to theorize about the principles concerning the *rate* and *accuracy* of comprehension that accompanies the rauding process. All processes have a time dimension, so the rate at which processes operate is of major interest. Consider the following principle:

Principle 5: Internal Articulation Rate. There is a certain fastest rate, in syllables per minute, at which an individual can internally articulate all the words and still be able to comprehend each consecutive thought.

There is purported to be a certain limiting rate at which the words used in sentences to express thoughts can be said to oneself and all of the other steps in the process still continue to function with success. Internal articulation facilitates the successful functioning of the rauding process (Principle 2), but there is purported to be a certain rate in syllables per minute beyond which the process cannot function successfully.

Let me interrupt myself at this point and give you a definition. *Rauding rate* is the highest rate at which an individual can raud a passage. Rauding rate is the maximum rate at which an individual can operate the rauding process on a passage with all or almost all of the consecutively encountered thoughts being comprehended. With this definition of rauding rate, I think you can see that Principle 5 holds that rauding rate is limited by a certain fastest rate at which the words in consecutively encountered sentences can be internally articulated and still be transformed into the thoughts the author intended to communicate.

Fran: By definition, rauding rate is the fastest rate at which a passage can be rauded, and by Principle 5 this rate is limited by how fast a person can say the words in passages and still raud the passage.

Carver: That's right. Notice that it would be impossible for the rauding rate of an individual to be higher than the very fastest rate at which a person could say all the words in a passage to himself/herself.

Fran: You mean that if you said all the words in a passage to yourself just as fast as possible, without bothering to try to comprehend the thoughts, then your rauding rate could not possibly be higher than this rate.

Carver: Exactly. The individual's rauding rate would have to be equal to or less than this rate. This means that rauding theory has restricted rauding to rates considerably below 1000 words per minute. The data I have seen suggest that individuals could not internally articulate all the words in a passage at a rate faster than about 500 words per minute. Therefore, I am saying that it would be impossible to find someone who could raud a passage faster than about 500 words per minute.

Fran: What if a passage was used that had been rauded previously?

Carver: I'm glad you asked that question. It has made me aware that I have failed to clarify that rauding theory is based upon individuals encountering passages that are new or unfamiliar. The passages must be unfamiliar in the sense that they have never been seen before. This is what ordinarily happens in the real world, and these are the situations with which rauding theory wants to deal. The content or subject matter may be familiar in the sense that the individual has no problem in rauding it, but the passage is still unfamiliar in the sense that the passage has never been encountered before.

Fran: Let's go back to rauding rate and internal articulation. Do you think that most people can raud a passage just as fast as they can say all the words to themselves?

Carver: No. Not at all. I think that processes that include extra steps or activities cannot possibly proceed as fast. Saying all the words to oneself as fast as possible with the added requirement that the words be transformed into thoughts, could not proceed as fast as when this additional requirement was not there.

I also think rauding rate will vary considerably between individuals due to individual differences in speed of mental functioning. It seems reasonable to me that some individuals will be able to raud faster than others. Some people can run faster than other people, and some people can count faster than other people. It seems reasonable that some people will have a higher rauding rate than other people because their speed of mental functioning is faster.

Fran: This factor sounds like an IQ variable.

Carver: It is like IQ in that it is a general ability factor that is not necessarily specific to reading. However IQ measurement ordinarily includes knowledge components and other nonspeed factors.

I'm talking about a speed of thinking factor that limits how fast an individual can perform the verbal gymnastics necessary to say the words in a sentence and transform them into the complete thought the author intended to communicate.

Fran: Let me try to summarize again. The fastest successful operation of the rauding process is called the rauding rate. You are theorizing that rauding rate is limited by how fast individuals can say the words to themselves and still think fast enough to continue to transform the sentences into the thoughts the author wanted to communicate. You are also saying that it seems to follow that (a) individuals have a maximum internal articulation rate that sets an upper limit on their rauding rate, and (b) individuals also vary with respect to how fast they can think through the steps of the rauding process; this also sets a limit upon their rauding rate.

Carver: Another excellent summary.

Fran: Is there anything else that influences the rauding process rate?

Carver: Yes, during reading, the eye movements become habituated and influence rate. Consider this principle:

> *Principle 6:* Eye Movements. During reading, when the eyes are moved at a constant rate for many hours, they become habituated at this rate.

Eye movements are theorized to be a psychomotor activity similar to walking. Each individual usually has a walking pace that is most comfortable; this rate is probably most efficient in that it maximizes speed and minimizes stress or recovery time at the end of the walk. This rate of walking has evolved over a period of time covering a great many hours of walking experience, and it becomes habitual. The walker does not devote much attention to decisions about how fast to move the feet. Also, where each foot will be placed is not thought about much except that holes in the path are rather automatically avoided.

Rauding theory holds that the walking process is not a bad model for the eye movements associated with the rauding process. If an individual tends to operate the rauding process at a constant rate for many hours, then the eye movements will take on a rate of movement that is habitual. Eventually, there will be little or no time devoted to thinking about the rate the eyes are moving or the exact place where the eyes will be moved. After habituation, the individual does not devote much attention to the eye movements and is not conscious of thinking about where each succeeding fixation will be located except that blanks between words are rather automatically avoided.

Fran: Are you saying that the eye movement rate depends upon the rauding process rate initially, but eventually the eyes will move at habitual rate of their own after a great deal of experience at one particular rate?

Carver: That's right. The eye movements will evolve into a rate of their own after hours of experience at a single or constant rate. After habituation, there may be occasions when an individual could operate a particular reading process more efficiently at a faster or slower rate, but the eye movements have taken on a rate of movement on their own and it may not be a simple matter to change this rate in response to changes from one reading process to another.

I have said all I want to say about rate. Let's move on to *rauding accuracy.*

Fran: I don't think you have told me yet what "rauding accuracy" is.

Carver: It is the accuracy of passage comprehension that accompanies the rauding rate. When the rauding process is operated on a passage at the rauding rate, the accuracy with which the passage is comprehended is called the rauding accuracy.

Fran: I think I need for you to explain to me what you mean by accuracy.

Carver: The accuracy of passage comprehension is the number of thoughts comprehended divided by the total number of thoughts presented by the author in the passage. When the rauding process has been operated at the rauding rate, the rauding accuracy would be the proportion of thoughts covered that were comprehended.

Fran: So, rauding accuracy means the proportion of the total thoughts encountered that were comprehended while the rauding process was operating at the rauding rate.

Carver: Yes, the principle to be considered now is as follows:

Principle 7: Accuracy. Rauding accuracy depends upon rauding difficulty and rauding ability.

Rauding difficulty is the level of passage difficulty, and an individual's *rauding ability* is the level of passage difficulty at which 75 percent of the thoughts can be comprehended. Rauding cannot occur, by definition, when rauding difficulty exceeds rauding ability because the accuracy of comprehension would be less than 75 percent. Principle 7, stated differently, holds that rauding accuracy depends upon what level of rauding ability the individual brings to the passage and upon what level of rauding difficulty the author wrote the passage. As was mentioned before, authors write passages to communicate with a certain part of the population. Seldom are passages written with the idea in mind that everyone who can raud something will attempt to raud the particular passage being written. An author implicitly assumes certain attributes associated with the potential rauding audience, such as background knowledge and rauding skill. These assumptions are thereupon translated into what level of vocabulary can be used, what things need to be explained in detail, and what things need not be explained at all. These assumptions are made — sometimes they are erroneous assumptions — so as to produce a passage that will communicate the thoughts of the author in a manner that can and will be rauded by the assumed reading audience. If the author is highly successful in the construction of the passage, then almost everyone in the targeted reading audience who decides to attempt to raud the passage will in fact raud it; the accuracy of the rauding process is likely to be greater than 75 percent for almost everyone who attempts to raud it. This means that what the individual brings to the passage, in terms of prior knowledge of the subject matter and facility with the vocabulary used by the author, is sufficient to allow the individual to understand each thought as it is encountered during the operation of the rauding process. Sometimes the individual does not have the relevant background experiences, prior knowledge, or familiarity with the terminology, so the passages cannot be rauded. Stated differently, sometimes the rauding ability level of the individual is not sufficiently above the rauding difficulty of the passage, so rauding accuracy is below 75 percent. We therefore say that the individual was not able to raud the passage.

There are obviously a host of subfactors that contribute to whether the individual brings enough to the page to match what the author has put on the page. I have simply summarized all those subfactors primarily associated with the individual by lumping them together and calling the result the rauding ability of the individual. I have simply summarized all these subfactors associated with the passage itself by lumping them together and calling the result the rauding difficulty of the passage.

Fran: That seems simple enough. Rauding accuracy depends upon the amount of rauding ability the individual brings to the passage as well as the amount of rauding difficulty the author put into the passage.

Carver: You've got it. That polishes off the principles of rauding theory.

Chapter 6

WHAT ARE THE LAWS OF RAUDING THEORY?

Carver: I will be explaining to you the laws of rauding theory using verbal statements as well as mathematical equations. In the equations, certain variables will be represented by symbols; for example, rauding rate will be symbolized as R_r.* For you to understand what these equations mean, you will need to know the meaning of each symbol used in each equation. Therefore, it will be necessary for me to begin by defining all the important variables in rauding theory.

Fran: I am willing to try to learn these symbols and equations. I should warn you though, I usually try to avoid this kind of mental effort.

Carver: I realize that most people suffer from varying amounts of "symbol shock." It does require an extra amount of effort. I must confess that I also try to avoid learning symbols when I am attempting to raud what other researchers have written. However, it will be impossible for me to avoid symbols. Some of the ideas in rauding theory would be even more difficult to express without the precision of symbols and mathematical formulations.

Fran: I suppose I am as ready as I will ever be for you to start.

Carver: The fundamental unit in the theory is the "thought." A "thought" is a primitive, undefined term much the same as a "point" is in geometry. I will depend upon a great deal of intuitive understanding as to what the concept "thought" means.

Fran: I do have a general idea as to what you mean by the thoughts contained in a passage. Yet, this unit is still very vague.

Carver: Later, I will tie down this theoretical concept, empirically. For now, please go along with me and consider a set of related sentences, called a passage, as containing a certain num-

---

* A List of Rauding Theory Symbols is included in the Appendices.

51

ber of thoughts. I will symbolize the number of thoughts in a passage as T_p.

Fran: Does T_p represent a count of these undefined things called thoughts?

Carver: Yes. A passage might contain 50 thoughts. Therefore, $T_p = 50$.

After an individual has been exposed to the thoughts in a passage, it is assumed that T_p can be divided into two portions. One portion consists of the thoughts that were comprehended, and the other portion consists of the thoughts that were not comprehended. The portion of thoughts that were comprehended will be symbolized as T_c. The portion of thoughts that were *not* comprehended will be symbolized as T_n.

Therefore, I hope you can see that

$$T_p = T_c + T_n. \tag{1}$$

Fran: You mean that if a person read a passage that contained fifty thoughts, then he or she might comprehend forty thoughts and not comprehend ten thoughts.

Carver: Right. In your example $T_p = 50$, $T_c = 40$, and $T_n = 10$. Using Equation 1, $50 = 40 + 10$.

Fran: I don't remember your talking about T_n in your original presentation.

Carver: I didn't. But, don't worry about that. I'm not adding T_n to change, but to clarify.

Any time you divide something into portions, it is often convenient to refer to proportions or percents instead of the actual numbers. For example, if a university class of students contains a total of 50 students, 40 female and 10 male, it is often convenient to say that the proportion of the class that was female was .80, which is 40/50. We may also multiply .80 by 100 to convert to percent and say that the class consisted of 80 percent females. Similarly, it will be convenient to say, for this example of yours, that the proportion of thoughts that were comprehended was T_c/T_p, or .80. This proportion will be called the accuracy of passage comprehension, and it will be symbolized as A. Put into a mathematical formula,* we can say that

---

* A List of Most Important Rauding Theory Equations is included in the Appendices.

$$A = \frac{T_c}{T_p}. \tag{2}$$

Now, if we take the number of thoughts in a passage, T_p, and divide by the total amount of time the passage was presented, the result will be called the rate of passage presentation. If we symbolize *presentation time* using t, and if we symbolize the rate of passage presentation using R, then we can say that

$$R = \frac{T_p}{t}. \tag{3}$$

Fran: Let me check my understanding of this. Suppose the reader I mentioned earlier was given the passage for 2 minutes. Would that mean

$$R = \frac{50}{2}$$

or that the rate of passage presentation was 25 thoughts per minute?

Carver: Right. There is one more important definition involving the preceding variables. The *efficiency* of passage presentation, symbolized as E, is the number of thoughts comprehended, T_c, divided by the presentation time, t. In equation form, the definition of the efficiency of passage comprehension is

$$E = \frac{T_c}{t}. \tag{4}$$

Fran: So, for my example

$$E = \frac{40}{2},$$

or the efficiency of passage comprehension for this hypothetical reader would be 20 thoughts per minute.

Carver: Yes. Let's review. A is the accuracy of passage comprehension. It is also the proportion of thoughts in a passage that has been comprehended, T_c/T_p.

R is the rate at which the passage has been presented. It is also T_p/t, the rate at which the passage is presented in thoughts per minute.

E is the efficiency of passage comprehension. It is also T_c/t, the rate at which the passage was comprehended in thoughts per minute.

Fran: I think I understand what you mean by these symbols, *now.* However, I may forget later.

Carver: I'll try to remember to keep reminding you.

Rauding rate, as I mentioned earlier, is symbolized by R_r. It is the maximum rate at which the rauding process can be successfully operated on passages that could be rauded at lower rates.

Rauding accuracy is symbolized as A_r. It is the accuracy of comprehension when the rauding process is operated at the rauding rate. It is also the proportion of the total thoughts in a passage that are comprehended when the rauding process is operated on the entire passage at the rauding rate.

E_r will be used to symbolize *rauding efficiency.* It is the efficiency of comprehension when the rauding process is operated at the rauding rate. It is also the number of thoughts in a passage that are comprehended divided by the time required to complete the passage at the rauding rate.

Do you have any questions about these definitions or symbols before I present to you the laws of rauding?

Fran: Later, I'll probably find out that I did not understand these definitions as well as I thought I did. But, for now, I guess you can proceed.

Carver: I'm now ready to present the laws of rauding theory. They have been patterned after Newton's famous three laws of motion. You have heard of name dropping and guilt by association. I could easily be accused of name dropping and an attempt to suggest greatness by association. Neither is intended; rather, I wanted to share with you part of the genesis of the three laws of rauding.

I'll write all three laws on the chalkboard and then we can talk about each one in turn. I'll also write Newton's three laws of motion beside them so you can more readily see how the three laws of motion stimulated the three laws of rauding. At the end of the verbal statement of each law, I will give you the law in its symbolic form.

Three Laws of Rauding

Law I. Individuals attempt to comprehend thoughts in passages at a constant rate, called the rauding rate, unless they are influenced by situation-specific factors to change that rate.
(R = R$_r$)

Law II. The efficiency of passage comprehension depends upon the accuracy of passage comprehension and the rate of passage presentation.
(E = AR)

Law III. The most efficient rate of comprehending thoughts in a passage is the rauding rate.
(When R = R$_r$, E$_{max}$ = E$_r$, or when R $\neq$ R$_r$, E < E$_r$)

Three Laws of Motion

Law I. Every body perseveres in its state of rest, or of uniform motion in a right line unless it is compelled to change that state by forces impressed thereon.
(v = k)

Law II. The alteration of motion is ever proportional to the motive force impressed; and is made in the direction of the right line in which that force is impressed.
(f = ma)

Law III. To every action there is always opposed an equal reaction; or the mutual actions of two bodies upon each other are always equal, and directed to contrary parts.
f = f')

Fran: I assume you do not expect me to spend a lot of time trying to raud Newton's Three Laws of Motion.

Carver: That's right. Also, you should not spend a great deal of time trying to figure out correspondences between the two sets of laws. The Three Laws of Rauding were not designed to be like the three laws of motion in every respect.

Fran: I've been trying to raud your Three Laws of Rauding, without as much success as I would like.

Carver: Let me see if I can help.

Law I is saying that individuals ordinarily operate their rauding process on a passage at the rauding rate unless there is something atypical about the situation. This means that each individual is purported to have a maximum rate at which the rauding process can be executed and that most people execute the rauding process at this rate.

Fran: Do you mean that most of the time when people are

reading they are executing the rauding process and that they will execute this process at a constant rate?

Carver: Yes. Furthermore, this constant rate of operating the rauding process will be R_r. Each person is purported to have a single value for R_r. Some people will have higher R_r values than others, as I discussed earlier, but R_r will be a constant for each person.

Fran: I don't think I see how you got this law or why you think it is valid.

Carver: Let's cover the rationale underlying the laws after you are sure you understand what each one is.

Fran: Okay, but, before you go on to the next one, can you give me an example of what you mean by situation-specific factors?

Carver: I mean those things that are responsible for why a person sometimes does other things, such as scanning, skimming, or memorizing, instead of attempting to raud a passage. For example, if I gave you a passage and asked you to "read" it, I would expect R to equal R_r; I would expect that the rate you would cover the passage, R, would be your rauding rate, R_r. However, if I gave you a passage and told you to tell me as quickly as you could how many times the word "a" was used in the passage, I would expect you to operate a scanning process. When scanning, I would not expect R to equal R_r. If I asked you to study a passage because I was going to ask you to write down everything in the passage you could remember when you were through, this would be a situation-specific factor that would be outside the realm of Law I. However, if I gave you a second passage and asked you to "read" it, I would expect you to cover it at the same rate as you did the first passage, and I would expect both rates to be equal to the rauding rate, R_r.

Fran: Okay, I think I understand Law I. The $R = R_r$ at the end means that ordinarily the rate that a person will complete a passage is that person's rauding rate.

Carver: Right. Let's go on to Law II. Some people will argue that Law II is more of a definition than a law. This is because of the way that E, A, and R were defined earlier. Notice that

$$E = AR \qquad (5)$$

because

$$\frac{T_c}{t} = \frac{T_c}{T_p} \times \frac{T_p}{t} \qquad (6)$$

It is sometimes difficult to discriminate between laws and definitions. For example, it has been argued by some people that Newton's laws may be considered as definitions. With respect to Law II of rauding theory, the intent of the law is to go somewhat beyond these definitions. The intent is to convey the idea that the efficiency with which a passage is comprehended will be directly dependent upon, be a direct product of, the rate that the passage was presented and the accuracy with which the passage was comprehended.

Fran: It would seem to me that it is more of a definition than a law.

Carver: I won't argue with you about that. Sometimes, it is relatively arbitrary what are called laws, principles, hypotheses, axioms, postulates, premises, etc.

Fran: Let me see if I can confirm your Law II for myself. Earlier I used an example where $T_p = 50$, $T_c = 40$, and $t = 2$. I found that $A = .80$, $R = 25$, and $E = 20$. By substituting the relevant values into your Equation 5, I should find that

$$20 = (.80)(25)$$

and it does. From your Equation 6, I should find that

$$\frac{40}{2} = \frac{40}{50} \times \frac{50}{2}$$

and it does.

Carver: Very good! I should also point out to you that since $E = AR$, it follows that

$$E_r = A_r R_r. \qquad (7)$$

This means that if your rauding rate is 25 thoughts per minute and your rauding accuracy for a passage is .80, then your rauding efficiency for the passage will be 20 thoughts per minute, i.e.

$$E_r = (.80)(25) = 20.$$

Let's move on to Law III. This law holds that the rauding rate, R_r, is the most efficient rate for operating the rauding process on a passage. Any rate that the passage is covered other than the rauding rate will result in a lower efficiency of passage comprehension, E, than would have occurred at the rauding rate.

Fran: That doesn't seem too difficult to follow, but I'd like for you to say some more about the symbolic form of the law.

Carver: There are two ways to express the law in symbolic form. The first one says that when a passage is covered at the rauding rate, $R = R_r$, then the highest or maximum possible efficiency of passage comprehension will be equal to the rauding efficiency, $E_{max} = E_r$. The second symbolic way of stating the law says that when a passage is not covered at the rauding rate, $R \neq R_r$, then the obtained efficiency of comprehension will be less than that which would occur at the rauding rate, $E < E_r$.

Fran: Could you give me an example or two?

Carver: All right. Let me give some values to these symbols so I can illustrate using concrete examples. But first let me make sure that you know that $=$ means *equals*, $\neq$ means *not equal*, and $E < E_r$ means E *less than* E_r.

Fran: I knew that!

Carver: Good. Now, let's say that I give you a passage that contains 100 thoughts, $T_p = 100$. Let's say that your rauding rate is 20 thoughts per minute, $R_r = 20$. How long would it take for you to finish the passage at your rauding rate?

Fran: If there are 100 thoughts and I cover them at the rate of 20 thoughts per minute, then it would take me 5 minutes to finish.

Carver: Right. Now let's say that this passage is not too difficult for you, so your rauding accuracy was .80, $A_r = .80$. What would your rauding efficiency be?

Fran: Well, $E_r = A_r R_r$ from Equation 7, so $E_r = (.80)(20)$, $E_r = 16$ thoughts per minute.

Carver: Right. So, in this situation we can say that $T_p = 100$, $R_r = 20$, $t_r = 5$, $A_r = .80$, and $E_r = 16$.

Fran: Is "t_r" the symbol you use for the time it takes to raud a passage at the rauding rate?

Carver: Yes, "t_r" symbolizes *rauding time*. It is the time it takes for an individual to complete a passage while operating the rauding process at the rauding rate. Remember, in this example you would comprehend sixteen thoughts per minute if you operate the rauding process on the passage at your rauding rate of twenty thoughts per minute. Now, the Third Law of Rauding says that if you attempt to raud that passage at another rate besides twenty thoughts per minute, then your efficiency will drop below sixteen. Stated differently, if you spend *more* than five minutes on the passage your efficiency will be less than sixteen thoughts comprehended each minute, and if you spend *less* than five minutes on the passage your efficiency will also be less than sixteen thoughts comprehended per minute. When you spend more than five minutes, then $t \neq t_r$ and $R \neq R_r$. When you spend less than five minutes, $t \neq t_r$ and $R \neq R_r$. That's what I meant when I said E would be less than E_r when R was not equal to R_r.

$$E < E_r \text{ when } R \neq R_r.$$

Or in this hypothetical situation of yours,

$$E < 16 \text{ when } R \neq 20.$$

When I said

$$E \text{ is at a maximum when } R = R_r,$$

I was saying that your efficiency would be at its highest, 16, when your rate, R, was equal to 20; any rate less than or greater than 20 would produce an efficiency less than 16.

Fran: You imply at all times that rauding accuracy, A_r, is not manipulatable. Did I miss something?

Carver: Rauding accuracy for a particular person who is attempting to raud a particular passage is *not* manipulatable. It is constant, not variable, in this situation. It is the proportion of the passage the individual would comprehend if the rauding process were to be executed on the passage, once, at the rauding rate. Rauding accuracy may vary within an individual from one passage to another passage.

Fran: I get it! I think I understand the three laws now.

Carver: Good. Now, let me see if I can help you understand how the three laws may be derived from the principles I discussed earlier. I'll start with Law III.

This law can be derived from what we know about efficiency and rauding rate. Rauding rate is the fastest rate that a passage can be rauded. Operating the rauding process at rates faster than this should produce a loss in efficiency of passage comprehension, and rates slower than this should also be less efficient. Increasing the rauding process rate beyond the rauding rate must be counterproductive in terms of thoughts comprehended per a unit of time because rates beyond the rauding rate must reduce thoughts comprehended precipitously. If an individual is comprehending all or almost all of the thoughts at the rauding rate, then decreasing the rauding process rate below the rauding rate also has to be counterproductive in terms of thoughts comprehended per a unit of time. Efficiency must be at a maximum when an individual is comprehending all or almost all of the thoughts in the shortest possible amount of time.

Fran: That gives me some background for how you came up with Law III. Law II simply says what seems to be rather obvious, given your definitions of the variables, that the efficiency of comprehension of a passage depends directly upon the product of accuracy and rate. What about Law I?

Carver: This law incorporates a number of theoretical ideas. It asserts that whenever a particular individual encounters a particular passage and desires to comprehend the thoughts in the passage, then the individual will operate the rauding process at a constant rate. If this particular individual encounters another passage and again desires to comprehend the thoughts in the passage, then this individual will again operate the rauding process at a constant rate; also, the rate for the second passage will be equal to the rate for the first passage. Furthermore, this constant rate within and between passages will be the rauding rate. The above conditions of this law will tend to hold under most circumstances, but there may be certain atypical situations where it would not be expected to hold.

The rationale for this law is quite extensive. First, let's cover the rationale for why it is held that the rauding process typically operates at the rauding rate. After we finish that rationale we will cover why it is held that this typical rate that the rauding process operates, the rauding rate, is constant.

Individuals typically operate the rauding process at the rauding rate because it is typically the most efficient rate. An important assumption underlying rauding theory is that individuals behave efficiently. This idea that people have a tendency to be efficient is not unique to rauding theory. The idea can be traced at least as far back as Leibnitz, who invented calculus. He thought that nature always provided the least amount of energy expenditure for the greatest amount of effect; he believed in the optimality of nature. I'm simply applying this idea to situations where people raud.

If people raud most of the time, then they must raud at the rauding rate to be most efficient. Rauding theory holds that most people do raud most of the time and that most people do behave in the most efficient way most of the time; therefore people will typically operate the rauding process at the rauding rate. The rauding rate is held to be an *optimal rate* for operating the rauding process because rates higher and lower result in less efficiency of passage comprehension. The rauding rate is also a threshold rate for executing the rauding process because any rate higher than this will result in a precipitous loss of thoughts comprehended.

Fran: You are saying that it does not make sense that a typical individual would execute the rauding process at any rate other than the highest rate at which the process could be executed and all or almost all of the thoughts still be understood.

Carver: Yes. The theory holds that the rauding rate is an optimal rate for most individuals most of the time they are operating the rauding process, and therefore it makes sense that individuals would choose to operate their rauding process most of the time at this rate.

Fran: You have said more than once that the rauding process typically or ordinarily operates at the rauding rate. I assume this means that sometimes the rate at which the rauding process operates is not equal to the rauding rate. Can you give me an example of this?

Carver: Sure. The most apparent example involves auding. My rauding process operates while you are talking to me, but the process is not operating at my rauding rate. If your words were typed up, I could raud them at a much faster rate. That is, I would raud them at my rauding rate, which is the fastest rate at which I can operate my rauding process and still comprehend the thoughts you intend to communicate. Any time that a person does not have control over the rate at which the words are presented, it is likely that the rauding process will be operating at a rate different from the rauding rate. Even when a person does have control of the rate, as ordinarily is the case during reading, some persons *may* execute the rauding process at a rate different from the rauding rate. I will get into these situations in more detail later when I talk again about eye movements. For now, suffice it to say that the rauding process may operate at a rate slower than the rauding rate and it may operate at a rate faster than the rauding rate. However, the rauding process typically operates at the rauding rate, and that is a law of rauding theory.

Fran: It seems to me that many people raud as much during auding as they do during reading. Therefore, is it correct for the theory to contend that "typically" the rauding process operates at the rauding rate, since people have no control over rate during auding?

Carver: A good point! Rauding theory is most appropriate for situations that involve the rauding of "passages," and these situations are mostly reading situations. Notice that Law I talks about "passages."

Fran: I think I understand now why Law I holds that the rauding process will typically operate at the rauding rate. Now, I am ready for your rationale for why this rate, the rauding rate, is constant.

Carver: Rauding rate is constant because of the bottleneck created by the fixed amount of time it takes for the process to operate — to perceive words, internally articulate them, and use the words to build a thought out of a sentence. The words will not be internally articulated faster than the rauding rate because the mental functioning, thinking, required to formulate the thoughts out of sentences cannot proceed any faster. There is a certain fixed amount of time that each person needs to operate this process, which is paced by the internal articulation rate in syllables per minute. Each person learns that by saying the words in inner speech at this rate, the efficiency of passage comprehension is maximized. The constant rhythm of the internal articulation of the syllables acts as a pace-setting mechanism for the process.

The constancy of the process is paced by the subvocalization rate, and the eyes are made to move down the line at a rate that allows each word to be perceived, internally articulated, and the thought formulated out of the sentence. Since most reading involves rauding, and most rauding proceeds at the constant rauding rate, it follows from Principle 7 that the eyes will become habituated to move at the rauding rate. This means that any time the individual is operating the rauding process, whether rauding or not, the eyes will tend to move at the rauding rate. Initially, the eyes move during the rauding process at a rate that is paced by the rauding rate. However, after a great deal of experience with this constant rate of eye movement, the eyes take on a habitual rate of their own. This rate tends to pace the rauding process and further serves to stabilize it.

Once the eye movements become habituated at this rauding rate, after hours and hours of experience, then they will proceed at this constant rate on almost all occasions when passages are encountered. This is because the rauding process can be operated at this rate without any of the distractions associated with thinking about where to move the eyes. Therefore, when an individual encounters a passage and the individual desires to understand the thoughts the author wanted to communicate, then this overlearned psychomotor habit associated with the eye movements will be put in motion. The eyes will move down a line at a constant rate without adjusting for any possible differences in the meaning or redundancy of the words. This overlearned and constant rate will be used because over time it has tended to be the most efficient rate for understanding the thoughts contained in most of the passages encountered. To change or adjust this rate would be counterproductive because this would require attention being paid to the eyes in place of attention being paid to understanding the thoughts represented by the words.

For typical individuals who are rauding, it would not make sense for them to try to change the rate of eye movements anyway. If they were to move faster they would likely exceed the limits imposed by the maximum internal articulation rate or the speed of mental functioning. If they were to move at a slower rate so as to increase thoughts understood, that would probably not be an efficient way of adjusting. This is because the lack of comprehension of sentences is probably more associated with lack of understanding a particular word or of the general idea. Slowing down the entire process so that slightly more time was spent on each word or syllable might be beneficial were it not for the distractions associated with paying attention to the eye movements. A more effective strategy would probably be (a) to stop the rauding process completely and ponder or problem solve when comprehension is lacking (this means to shift to a studying process), and/or (b) regress to the beginning of a prior sentence and start the normal execution of the regular rauding process again in hopes that a second trial would be more successful.

I am trying to build a case for why Law I is valid from two standpoints. First, it makes sense from the standpoint of the principles and ideas already discussed. Second, alternative courses of action that are contrary to the law seem to be less reasonable than the course of action indicated by the law.

Fran: I think I understand how you derived these laws. Yet, if you don't mind saying some of these things again, perhaps in a different way, I think I would benefit from the redundancy.

Carver: Let me go over the typical situation again, and then I'll talk about an atypical situation to further explain the laws of rauding theory.

Most people raud the written material they encounter. The rauding process is most typically operated on this material at the rauding rate. The eye movements become habituated from a great deal of experience with the rauding process. Since the eye movements habitually move at the rate of the rauding process and since the rauding process typically operates at the rauding rate, this means that the eye movements automatically move at the rauding rate.

What I have just described is the typical situation. It includes all of those people in the world who raud almost all the time they read. However, let's take a look at what the theory would predict would happen for people who are atypical.

Suppose there are some people who do not raud most of the time they read. Suppose there are people who study most of the time they read because they are faced with extremely difficult to understand material. The theory would hold that their eye movements would become habituated at a studying process rate that is slower than the rauding rate. Now if these persons are given material that they can easily raud, they will attempt to execute the rauding process, but it will not likely be highly efficient because it will proceed at the rate and pattern set by the eye movements that became habituated during the studying process.

Likewise, a person who skims almost all the time instead of rauding is apt to have habituated the eye movements to a skimming process rate that is higher than the rauding rate. If this type of individual is then presented with a situation where it is best to execute the rauding process, it will not be easy for the individual to do this. The eye movements will have become habituated at a rate faster than the rauding rate, so it will likely require special attention to the eyes for the rauding process to function at a rate equal to the rauding rate. This type of distraction will not make the rauding process function as effectively as it would if the individual's eye movements had not become habituated at a skimming process rate that was higher than the rauding rate.

Fran: So, your theory is that eye movements can become habituated at rates other than the rauding rate. But you also contend that for almost all readers, the rauding process proceeds at the rauding rate automatically because the eyes have become habituated to raud at the rauding rate.

Carver: Correct.

Fran: I think I now understand how you derived your three laws. Later, I'll be looking closely at the empirical evidence that supposedly supports the laws. For now, I'm puzzled about one thing. It seems to me that data exist which show that children tend to read faster, on the average, each year they progress in school. How does your theory handle these changes in reading rate? Law I indicates a constancy of rauding rate. How does a constant rauding rate get changed?

Carver: Superficially, this does appear to be an inconsistency in rauding theory.

It is theorized that such changes in rauding rate are very

gradual and occur over long periods of rauding experience. As the child matures, speed of mental functioning is assumed to gradually increase, and there are likely to be gradual increases in maximum internal articulation rate also. It is assumed that the eye movements do not proceed at a perfectly constant rate but that there is a certain average rate with a normally distributed amount of variation around this average rate. When a student's rauding rate has increased, due to maturational factors, so that it is higher than the average habitual pace of the eye movements, it is assumed that a feedback mechanism operates. This mechanism should be similar in many ways to what happens with the walking rate of children. As they get older they tend to walk at a faster pace on the average because they find that when they walk slightly faster they do not experience the negative consequences that they had earlier. Over a great deal of time and experience their habitual walking rate gradually increases. Similarly, whenever the eye movements happen to go slightly faster and there are no negative consequences associated with efficiency of comprehension, then this behavior tends to be reinforced in a manner consonant with operant learning theory.

Fran: So you are saying that Law I predicts a relative constancy of rate for periods of time covering days, weeks, and months but not necessarily years.

Carver: Exactly.

Fran: Your laws are intriguing, to say the least. They also seem plausible. However, I've been around enough research to see that what seems reasonable before data collection frequently becomes unreasonable after data collection. Yet, I'm more interested now than I was before in seeing exactly what data there are that you think support these laws.

Carver: I'm glad that you are ready and eager to look at the data I have collected. These data are relevant to four hypotheses that have been derived from the Three Laws of Rauding.

Chapter 7

HAVE THE HYPOTHESES OF RAUDING THEORY RECEIVED SUPPORT?

Carver: There are many hypotheses that can be deduced from the principles and laws of rauding theory. I will only attempt to tell you about four major hypotheses that seem to enjoy especially strong empirical support at the present time.

My elaboration upon the hypotheses of rauding theory and their supporting data will be quite lengthy. It will help you, I think, if I start out by giving you an overview of the main things I want to talk about. The first hypothesis will deal with the typical constancy of reading rate. The second hypothesis is concerned with the efficiency of reading and auding. The third and fourth hypotheses are quantitative and will be expressed in the form of mathematical equations. Either one of us may elect to digress at times, but these four hypotheses will constitute the core of what I would like to explain to you.

Hypothesis 1

Fran: You said you were going to begin with a hypothesis about the constancy of reading rate. I assume that means that the hypothesis has been derived from Law I.

Carver: Right. You will remember that the prime stimulus for the original work on rauding theory was the finding that rate did not decrease with increases in the difficulty of the material. Instead, rate was relatively constant for the three easiest passages and only dropped off for the most difficult passage. It is relatively easy for rauding theory to explain this empirical result. The individuals were rauding the three easiest passages and that is why their rate was stable or constant; the First Law of Rauding readily explains this constancy of rate. The drop-off in rate for the most difficult passage indicates that the individuals were not able to raud this passage. Instead of continuing to operate the rauding process when they encountered sentences they could not understand, they probably went back and tried to figure out the meaning of the words and sentences. In short, they were probably shifting back and forth between the rauding process and a studying process.

The preceding explanation involves a hypothesis that follows from the First Law of Rauding. It is as follows: *Ordinarily, individuals will read at a constant rate even when the passages vary considerably in difficulty, as long as the rauding difficulty of the passages does not exceed the rauding ability of the individuals.*

A study was conducted to test this hypothesis. Students from Grade 4 through college were given passages and asked to read them normally. They were told that there would be no test on what they read because the researcher only wanted to find out approximately how fast people normally read. The passages were selected to represent the following grade level difficulties: Grade 1, Grade 4, Grade 7, Grade 10, Grade 13, and Grade 16. The students were allowed one minute to read the material at each of these six grade levels, and they were instructed to circle the word they were reading when they were told to stop. From these data, reading rate was determined.

Reading rate was not derived by counting each word that was read during the minute. You may remember that this procedure does not control for word length; words vary considerably in length and the more difficult the passage the longer the words, on the average. To provide a test of rauding theory, you might think it would be best to measure rate in syllables per minute, since internal articulation is what is supposed to pace the rauding process. However, this was not done, because it is an unnecessary nuisance to have to count syllables. Other research has already shown an almost perfect correlation between the number of syllables per word in passages and the number of letters per word in passages. Rate measured in syllables per minute is an almost perfect linear function of the number of letters per second, or character spaces per minute. Therefore, rate was measured using six letter spaces as a standard length word so that rate could be reported in standard length words per minute.

For each person a count was made of the number of letters in words and the number of spaces between words, including punctuation, from the beginning of the material to the word that was circled at the end of one minute. This total count of letter spaces was then divided by six to give the number of standard length words read in one minute. Standard length words per minute is symbolized by "Wpm" — note the capitalized "W" and lower case "p" and "m."

When rate was measured in *Words per minute*, Wpm, it was found that there was little or no change in rate from one grade level of difficulty to another. The 435 students whose data were analyzed for this research study were divided into rauding ability levels according to their scores on a reading test that had been administered prior to this reading rate study. It was found, for example, that even the students who were at a college level of rauding ability tended to read all of these passages at a relatively constant rate. The average rates for the Grade 4, Grade 7, Grade 10, and Grade 13 materials varied only between 290 and 310 Wpm for these students who tested out at the college level of rauding ability. They read the Grade 1 material *slightly* faster, 325 Wpm, and they slowed down somewhat to about 250 Wpm for the Grade 16 materials. Yet, the Grade 16 passage was higher than the rauding ability of this group of individuals; their rauding ability level ranged between Grade 13 and Grade 15.

For the individuals who were at levels of rauding ability below the college level, their rates were even more constant than the college level individuals. In fact, these lower ability individuals tended to maintain a constant average rate even when the rauding difficulty of the passage exceeded their own rauding ability. This data analysis provided strong support for Hypothesis 1.

These data from this rate study were analyzed another way to provide additional evidence relevant to Hypothesis 1. It was determined how much the individuals changed their rates, up or down, from one level of difficulty to another as long as the rauding difficulty of the material was not at a level that was higher than their own rauding ability. It was found, for example, that the college level group that we just discussed changed their rates, on the average, only about 16.4 percent. This means, for example, that their rate for reading the Grade 13 material was only about 16 percent different from their rate for reading the

Grade 4 material, on the average. From these data, it appears that younger readers as well as mature readers tend to read at a relatively constant rate even if the difficulty of the material changes drastically. Thus, these two analyses of the Study I data, as well as previously collected data that I will not review at this time, seem to provide strong support for the first hypothesis. In turn, direct support for this particular hypothesis lends indirect support for the First Law of Rauding.

These data that I have just reviewed for you have not yet been published, so I will give you this copy of the submitted manuscript and ask you to raud it in your leisure time.[1] If you have questions or comments about these data or this research, I would be glad to deal with them later. Do you have anything to say before we move on to the next hypothesis?

Fran: Just a comment. It seems rather obvious that it would be difficult to patch up rauding theory if the constancy of the rate that typical people read ran into trouble from an empirical standpoint.

Carver: Definitely! If you want to attack rauding theory at its most crucial point, you should go after the First Law of Rauding and the hypotheses that may be derived from it. You will notice that I did *not* say, "its most vulnerable point." I do not think you will have much success in trying to show that, typically, individuals do not raud at a constant rate, because the existing data and the present theoretical rationale seem especially sound to me.

Fran: But what about all of the talk in reading circles about mature readers being flexible readers?

Carver: I have two reactions to this. First raud the research paper I just gave you and all of the other empirical data and theory relevant to reading flexibility and see what you conclude on your own. Second, I think flexibility is a fine thing if flexibility means knowing when to shift gears from one processing mode to another. Obviously, if a student needs to understand the material in a difficult textbook and be able to recall it to pass a test in a course, then the student should know how and when to switch

---

1. Ronald P. Carver, "Is Reading Rate Constant or Flexible?"

from the operation of the rauding process to a studying process and to a memorizing process. If an individual has a job that requires some knowledge about a great deal of information, such as technical reports, the individual should know how and when to switch back and forth from a skimming process to the rauding process. If this is what flexibility means, I am all for it. However, if flexibility does *not* mean gear shifting from one processing mode to another but instead means the automatic and continual changing of rate *within* the rauding process, then I have to be shown because I was born and raised in Missouri! I ask, where are the data to support the existence of such flexibility?

Fran: Okay! Okay! You're getting carried away again, Professor Carver. My guess is that if I found data that seemed to support flexibility in the sense of a changing rauding process rate, you would try to find something wrong with the research.

Carver: You're probably right, but you show me the data first and we will worry about my possible biases and vested interests later.

Fran: Maybe someday I will. For now I'm willing to assume that your research, as well as other published data that I haven't read yet, supports your case well enough to justify investing more of my time trying to understand rauding theory.

Carver: Thank you, Fran, for your show of tentative faith. Let's move on to the second hypothesis.

Hypothesis 2

Carver: If the Third Law of Rauding is valid, then it should be possible to vary the rates that people are allowed to read printed material and find that there is in fact a rate where efficiency is at a maximum. The same should also hold true for auding. Hypothesis 2 will deal with this situation.

Fran: I have an idea of how you might vary the rate for printed material, but how would you vary auding rate?

Carver: Using time-compressed speech. This involves a piece of equipment that allows passages that are tape recorded at a comfortable speaking rate to be speeded up. Small pieces of the tape are chopped out, figuratively but not literally. The tape plays the words back faster with tiny pieces removed, but you do not get as much of the Donald Duck effect as you get when you simply speed up a record or tape. In time-compressed speech, the tape is not played at a faster rate, it simply appears to be played at a faster rate. It has been shortened or compressed by removing small parts, which makes the remaining parts closer together. This type of equipment allows you to produce auditory rates that are comparable to a wide range of reading rates, for example, from 150 wpm to 450 wpm.

Fran: Okay, from the Third Law of Rauding you are deducing that both in the reading mode and the auding mode there should be a rate where the efficiency of the rauding process is at a maximum.

Carver: Yes. Furthermore, it follows from the principles of rauding theory and the Third Law of Rauding that the most efficient rate for comprehending thoughts during reading and during auding will be exactly the same rate.

Fran: Why?

Carver: Well, it has to be this way because the Third Law of Rauding is a general law that should cover both reading and auding. It states that the most efficient rate of comprehending thoughts is the rauding rate. Thus, the rauding rate of individuals will be the most efficient rate for comprehending thoughts during reading, and exactly this same rate will be the most efficient rate during auding. Therefore, if we find, in fact, that reading has a rate that is *most* efficient and auding also has a rate that is *most* efficient, then it follows that they must be the same rate because both of these most efficient rates are caused by the same factor, the rauding rate.

Fran: I understand now. But could you state this second hypothesis more explicitly?

Carver: I'd be glad to. But before I do, let me remind you of a term I used earlier in our discussion, optimal rate. The rate that is associated with maximum efficiency would be an optimal rate in that it is the rate that optimizes or maximizes efficiency. Therefore, rauding rate is also an optimal rate, since it is the rate where the most thoughts are understood per a certain amount of time.

Now, I can state the second hypothesis quite simply as follows: *The optimal rate for comprehending thoughts while reading equals the optimal rate while auding.* The data that were collected to test this hypothesis were strongly supportive. Now, let me describe the data. I will call the earlier research paper I gave you, on the constancy of reading rate, Study I. This second one I'm handing to you now, I will call Study II.[2]

Study II involved 102 college students who were presented passages at four levels of difficulty, Grade 5, Grade 8, Grade 11, and Grade 14; the passages were presented both visually and auditorily. There were twenty passages at each of the four grade levels of difficulty. Ten of the twenty passages at each level of difficulty were read and ten were auded. The ten reading passages were presented at exactly the same ten rates as the ten auding passages. Rate was controlled in the reading mode using motion picture film. Rate was controlled in the auding mode by use of the time-compressed speech technique I described to you earlier. The ten rates varied from 83 Wpm to 500 Wpm. There were two kinds of objective tests on the passages — two objective ways to measure passage comprehension — and there was also a subjective rating by the individual of how much of a passage was comprehended at each rate.

No matter which of the three methods was used to measure accuracy of comprehension of the passages, the results turned out almost exactly the same. When the efficiency of comprehension was estimated by multiplying the accuracy scores by the rate, $E = AR$, it was found that (a) efficiency was at a maximum around 300 Wpm for the reading mode, and (b) efficiency was at a maximum around 300 Wpm for the auding mode. Furthermore, this same 300 Wpm optimal rate for the reading and 300 Wpm optimal rate for auding occurred at each of the four levels of difficulty.

Let me make my point another way that is longer but should be clearer. For the Grade 5 passages, the optimal rate of reading was approximately 300 Wpm and the optimal rate of auding was approximately 300 Wpm. For the Grade 8 passages, the optimal

---

2. Ronald P. Carver, "Optimal Rate of Reading Prose."

rate of reading was approximately 300 Wpm and the optimal rate of auding was approximately 300 Wpm. For the Grade 11 passages, the optimal rate of reading was approximately 300 Wpm and the optimal rate of auding was approximately 300 Wpm. For the Grade 14 passages, the optimal rate of reading was 300 Wpm and the optimal rate of auding was 300 Wpm.

From these data, it seems reasonable to claim strong support for Hypothesis 2 that the optimal rate for comprehending thoughts during reading is equal to the optimal rate for auding. Furthermore, these data lend strong indirect support to the Third Law of Rauding from which the hypothesis was derived. Also, it should not escape your attention that these Study II data provide additional strong support for the First Law of Rauding. It would be possible for the optimal rate for reading to equal the optimal rate for auding at each difficulty level, but the optimal rate might be different at different difficulty levels. Indeed, this is what conventional wisdom about reading would have pre-dicted — that the most efficient rate at Grade 14 would be lower than the most efficient rate at Grade 5. If the optimal rate of reading was 300 Wpm at Grade 14, why wasn't it 350 Wpm or higher, for example, at Grade 5? A mature reader is supposed to be flexible, at least that is what I perceive as conventional wisdom. If conventional wisdom is correct, then why couldn't these college students, who should be among the best readers in the world, change their processing rates so that their most efficient rate at Grade 5 was higher than it was at Grade 14? The predictions from conventional wisdom *were not* verified; the predictions made from rauding theory *were* verified. Thus, these data from Study II provide strong support for the existence of a rauding rate that is relatively constant in typical reading situations and is the most efficient rate at which the student can comprehend thoughts during reading and auding; this means strong support for Law I and Law III. Also, these techniques for collecting efficiency data relevant to Law III depend somewhat upon the validity of Law II, $E = AR$. So, this direct empirical support we find for Law III also reflects indirect support for Law II. It appears that Study II provides empirical support for all three laws.

I will summarize what I have covered so far. Hypothesis 1 and Hypothesis 2 were derived from the Three Laws of Rauding and have received strong empirical support in Studies I and II. In turn, these results reflect support for all three Laws of rauding theory.

Now, you should be better able to understand why I had the audacity to refer to the three *laws* of rauding theory.

Fran: I am duly impressed by what you have told me. Still, when I get around to my attempt to raud the Study II research report, I will probably be looking for loopholes or reasons why things aren't nearly as neat as you have interpreted them to be.

Carver: This is as it should be in the kingdom of science. I will welcome your careful and critical rauding of Study II. If I have made illogical inferences, please don't let me continue down a deadend path without warning me. On the other hand, if you do not find crucial problems with these theoretical ideas and their associated empirical data, then I hope you will consider joining me in testing the theory further. But I'm getting too far ahead. We still have more hypotheses and data to cover.

Hypothesis 3

Carver: Let's move now to Hypothesis 3, which is the first quantified hypothesis of rauding theory. In those reading situations where the First Law of Rauding holds, the person will start the operation of the rauding process at the beginning of the passage and continue to the end of the passage; the proportion of thoughts in the passage that were comprehended would be A_r; $A = A_r$. In that hypothetical example I gave you earlier, A_r equalled .80.

Fran: I remember.

Carver: Good. Do you remember how many thoughts there were in that example passage?

Fran: 100, or $T_p = 100$.

Carver: If $A_r = .80$ and $T_p = 100$, what would T_c equal when you are operating the rauding process at the rauding rate?

Fran: That would be .80 × 100 or 80. I also remember that it took me five minutes to complete the passage at the rauding rate, $t_r = 5$.

Carver: Okay, suppose I had stopped you after two minutes of rauding. Could you estimate how many thoughts you would have comprehended at that point?

Fran: Let me talk my way through this. If it takes me five minutes to cover 100 thoughts, in two minutes I should have covered about two-fifths of 100 or forty thoughts. But, you asked me how many I had comprehended, not how many I had covered, so that would be two-fifths of eighty or about thirty-two thoughts.

Carver: Right. Now let me give you an equation that symbolizes in summary form the relationships you used to solve this problem.

$$T_c = \frac{t}{t_r} (A_r T_p) \tag{8}$$

$$T_c = (2/5) (.80 \times 100) = (2/5) (80) = 32$$

Fran: You let t be the 2 minutes I was allowed to read?

Carver: Yes. That was your presentation time, $t = 2$. This equation expresses exactly the problem as you solved it. However, it will be convenient to rearrange some of the variables into other orders. You can see that

$$R_r = \frac{T_p}{t_r} \tag{9}$$

and

$$R_r = 100/5 = 20,$$

so you can also see that we can solve Equation 9 for rauding time,

$$t_r = \frac{T_p}{R_r}, \tag{10}$$

and

$$t_r = 100/20 = 5.$$

Rauding time was five minutes. If we substitute T_p/R_r for t_r in Equation 7, we have another way of estimating the number of thoughts you would have understood during the first two minutes. From Equation 8 and Equation 10,

$$T_c = \frac{t}{T_p/R_r} (A_r T_p) \tag{11}$$

and

$$T_c = A_r R_r t,$$ (12)

so

$$T_c = (.80)(20)2 = 32.$$

If you have trouble following this, it is solely because you are rusty with your algebra. These are simply substitutions with cancellation and rearrangement of terms. If you do not wish to bother with verification of what I am doing, you may simply have faith in my integrity and competency with mathematical equations.

Fran: I think I'll rely on the latter, but I appreciate your attempt to make it as simple as you can.

Carver: Equation 12 is a quantified hypothesis about how many thoughts you would comprehend if you were attempting to raud a passage at your rauding rate and you had a rauding accuracy of .80 for the passage. This means that if you were allowed to finish the passage, your accuracy would have been .80 because you would have comprehended 80 of the 100 sentences. Notice that I said that we would estimate T_c if you were *stopped short* of completion. The statement of Equation 12 needs to be refined so that it is properly qualified with respect to this time restriction, that is,

$$T_c = A_r R_r t \text{ when } t \le t_r.$$ (12)

Fran: You are saying that this hypothesized relationship between the number of thoughts an individual will comprehend in a passage and the amount of time the individual is allowed to raud the passage will only be valid as long as the presentation time is less than or equal to the rauding time.

Carver: That's correct.

Fran: Do you intend for this hypothesis to apply to passages of *any* length?

Carver: A passage would have to be at least one sentence long. However, it is questionable whether rauding theory should be tested with one-sentence passages, because in research situations it is sometimes possible to memorize a single sentence when presentation time equals rauding time.

Now, I want to get back to a further elaboration of the quantified hypothesis in Equation 12. We let the accuracy, A, of the comprehension of a passage be

$$A = \frac{A_r R_r t}{T_p} \tag{13}$$

or

$$A = (A_r R_r) \frac{t}{T_p}, \tag{14}$$

and

$$A = (80)(20) \frac{(2)}{(100)} = .32.$$

So the accuracy of comprehension of the entire passage, if we stopped you after two minutes, would be .32 or 32 percent of the thoughts in the passage would have been comprehended after two minutes. Equation 14 can be further rearranged by making use of

$$R = \frac{T_p}{t} \qquad \text{from Equation (3)}$$

so

$$\frac{t}{T_p} = \frac{1}{R}. \tag{15}$$

Notice that the quantity $1/R$ is the amount of time per thought presented. By substituting $1/R$ for t/T_p in Equation 14 we have

$$A = (A_r R_r) \frac{1}{R} \text{ when } R \geq R_r. \tag{16}$$

This equation says that when R is greater than or equal to the rauding rate, R_r, then the accuracy of the comprehension of a passage is equal to the product of the quantity $A_r R_r$ and $1/R$. Equation 16 will only hold when R is the average rate of overall rate that the passage was presented — when $1/R$ is the average amount of time each thought is presented. Thus in our hypothetical situation

$$R = \frac{100}{2} = 50 \qquad \text{from Equation (3)}$$

and

$$A = (.80)(20) \cdot \frac{1}{50} = .32, \text{ from Equation (16).}$$

Fran: You are about to put me to sleep, Professor. Where are you going?

Carver: I'm trying to give you some familiarity with Equation 16; it represents a quantified linear hypothesis that has been tested.

Hypothesis 3 may be stated either as

$$T_c = A_r R_r t \text{ when } t \leq t_r \quad \text{from Equation (12),}$$

or as

$$A = A_r R_r \frac{1}{R} \text{ when } R \geq R_r, \text{from Equation (16).}$$

However, I prefer to express the third hypothesis in the form of Equation 16 because it expresses the accuracy of comprehension of a passage, A, as a function of the time per thought, $1/R$, that the passage is presented. In verbal form, the third hypothesis is as follows: *The accuracy with which an individual comprehends a passage is equal to the product of the individual's rauding accuracy, rauding rate, and the amount of time per thought presented, provided that the average rate is greater than or equal to the rauding rate.*

Fran: It seems to me that I vaguely remember your referring to the relationship expressed in Equation 16 as "hyperbolic," in your original presentation.

Carver: I did, and that may be confusing. Equation 16 represents a hyperbolic relationship between A and R, and it also represents a linear relationship between A and $1/R$. Let me go on now to show you the linear side of this relationship. Suppose I gave you five 100-thought passages that were equal in difficulty, and everything else was the same as for that hypothetical situation we talked about earlier; $A_r = .80$ and $R_r = 20$. Suppose on the first passage I stopped you after one minute and on the second I stopped you after two minutes, and so on up until the fifth passage, on which I stopped you after five minutes. I'd like for you to calculate your accuracy of passage comprehension for each passage.

Fran: Okay. My five R values, using Equation 3, and five $1/R$ values would be

$$R_1 = \frac{100}{1} = 100 \quad \text{and} \quad \frac{1}{R_1} = .01$$

$$R_2 = \frac{100}{2} = 50 \quad \text{and} \quad \frac{1}{R_2} = .02$$

$$R_3 = \frac{100}{3} = 33.3 \text{ and} \quad \frac{1}{R_3} = .03$$

$$R_4 = \frac{100}{4} = 25 \quad \text{and} \quad \frac{1}{R_4} = .04$$

$$R_5 = \frac{100}{5} = 20 \quad \text{and} \quad \frac{1}{R_5} = .05$$

So, from Equation 16 my 5 A values would be

$$A_1 = (.80)\,(20)\,(.01) = .16$$
$$A_2 = (.80)\,(20)\,(.02) = .32$$
$$A_3 = (.80)\,(20)\,(.03) = .48$$
$$A_4 = (.80)\,(20)\,(.04) = .64$$
$$A_5 = (.80)\,(20)\,(.05) = .80$$

Carver: Very good! Now let's plot these A values as a function of $1/R$. Look at Figure 1 which I'll put on the chalkboard. Notice that the more time you are given to raud the passage, amount of time per thought, or $1/R$, the more of the passage you will comprehend, at least until you are able to finish the passage once at your rauding rate. The relationship between A and $1/R$ is a straight line that has a slope equal to the product of A_r and R_r, and an intercept of 0. Remember from your algebra that the intercept is the value of Y when X is 0. In this case, the value of A is 0 when $1/R$ is 0. This means that if I give you 0 minutes per each thought in the passage, you will not comprehend any of the passage; $A = 0$. The slope tells you how much of a gain there will be in thoughts comprehended when we allow you to attempt to raud for one full minute. In this case you will comprehend sixteen thoughts each minute you are given; the slope is 16, since $E_r = A_r R_r$ ($A_r R_r = 16$, and $E_r = 16$).

Again, this quantitative hypothesis may be stated differently as follows: *the proportion of a passage comprehended is linearly related to the amount of time allowed for rauding the passage, as long as the*

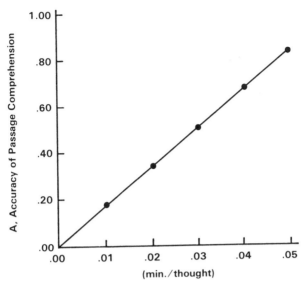

Figure 1.

presentation time does not exceed the rauding time. This hypothesis may be tested by administering passages that are approximately equal in difficulty for varying lengths of time and then seeing if the amount of comprehension of each passage is linearly related to the amount of time allowed for rauding.

Fran: I suppose you have Study III all ready to show me, which provides strong support for this hypothesized linear relationship between A and $1/R$.

Carver: I am slightly embarrassed to say that I do not. This is a loophole, so to speak, in building the case for strong empirical support for the rauding theory. Study III, which I will give you later, does contain data that provide empirical support for Hypothesis 3. However, Study III was not designed to test this hypothesis, so it should not be surprising that the study is not definitive in this respect.[1] You need to raud Study III and look carefully at the figure in it that presents the relationship between the ACCURACY OF COMPREHENSION and the TIME ALLOWED FOR READING. Then I think you will probably

1. Ronald P. Carver, "Reading Comprehension Under Normal and Speed Reading Conditions."

agree that the data provide support for the hypothesis that the relationship between A and $1/R$ is linear. Of course, there is no reason to expect this linear relationship to continue beyond the time allowed to finish rauding the passage once at the rauding rate.

Fran: I am genuinely surprised that you are not going to contend that there is strong evidence for this hypothesis.

Carver: I will surprise you again by claiming that I have seen a great deal of evidence that strongly supports this hypothesis.

Fran: I'm confused!

Carver: I have collected a great deal of data in pilot studies, and I have reanalyzed previously published data that have convinced me beyond a reasonable doubt that this hypothesis has wide empirical support. Unfortunately, none of these data are in publishable form at the present time.

Fran: From what I have learned in the research courses that I have taken from you, I must say that I am disappointed. How can I evaluate research that you will not or cannot show me?

Carver: I'm saying that I have seen enough empirical data to convince me that there should be little or no problem collecting data in the future that will convince you and others that there is strong empirical support for this hypothesis. In the meantime, I will call upon your own powers of reasoning to analyze this situation. Just think a minute. Do you really question that I would have a difficult time collecting empirical data showing that the more time I allowed you to operate your rauding process on a passage, the more of the passage you would comprehend, as long as I did not give you enough time to finish the passage? If you agree with this, then it is reasonable to expect a linear relationship between the accuracy of passage comprehension and the time allowed for rauding.

Fran: That does seem reasonable. On the other hand, I know that it is often difficult to collect data that support hypotheses that seem extremely straightforward and unassailable.

Carver: I agree. However, I do have data that support this hypothesis except they are not quite as extensive or overwhelming, or unassailable, as what I have been able to show you before. It was only when I began to talk to you and present things more from a rationalistic standpoint that it occurred to me that this hypothesis was readily deduced from the principles and laws, but it was one that I had taken for granted because I had already seen so much data that supported it. Yet, there was no way I could put all of those data together in a research report and present it to you.

Fran: I accept your apologies, but I will be on a close lookout to see what the future brings relevant to this hypothesis. There is one aspect of it that I would like for you to explain better. A is equal to zero when the time allowed for reading the passage is zero. Yet, we know that most people will be able to score higher than zero on almost any comprehension test that can be constructed even if they are not allowed any time to raud the passage.

Carver: I'm glad you brought that up because this is a point that has been misunderstood before and deserves further explanation. You are pointing out that the theory contends that A equals 0 when $1/R$ equals 0, yet you know that, in practice, empirical indicants of A are seldom equal to zero when the time allowed for reading is zero. My contention is that this is simply a scaling problem. By analogy, it is similar to changing from the z-score scale, which has a mean of 0 and a standard deviation of 1, to a T-score scale which has a mean of 50 and a standard deviation of 10. We haven't changed anything of substance when we change from one scale to the other, yet the numbers change drastically; the z-score scale usually has a number of zero or near zero scores, while the T-score scale almost never has a zero or near zero score. To test rauding theory, my contention is that we simply have to convert the empirical data to another scale that does not change the substance of the scores but does change the scale so that when time is zero the scores tend to be zero or near zero.

Study III, which I mentioned earlier, contains data that support the case that comprehension is in fact zero when time is zero — $A = 0$ when $t = 0$ — even though objective test scores tend not to be zero when $t = 0$.

Fran: I still don't believe I fully understand what you are trying to tell me.

Carver: I'll try to explain it again another way. Surely it is not too difficult to concede that if I give you no time to read a passage, $1/R = 0$, then you will not comprehend any of the thoughts in the passage, so $A = 0$.

Fran: There is no problem there.

Carver: All right, if you take a test on a passage that you have *not* been allowed to read prior to taking the test, then you may do better than zero on the test just because I am not perfect in making a measure of how many thoughts you have comprehended.

Fran: True enough.

Carver: The only thing left is for you to concede that this is simply a measurement problem or a scaling problem that can be handled in a manner similar to changing T scores into z scores.

Fran: This is the part that I'm not sure I quite understand.

Carver: I think I could explain this to you if I used a concrete example. However, it will be more convenient if I do this later when I cover measurement problems in general and scaling problems in particular. Would you let me postpone further explanation on this point until later?

Fran: I suppose.

Carver: I can see that you are lukewarm about putting this off, but I promise not to forget your concern.

Hypothesis 4

Carver: Before I proceed, I want to warn you that we have reached the end of the line in terms of major hypotheses that can be deduced from the principles and laws of rauding theory and also enjoy empirical support. I shall continue the discussion by telling you about empirical support for the fourth and final hypothesis. However, this particular hypothesis has not been derived from principles and laws. Instead, this second quantified hypothesis that I am about to present to you is an empirical generalization from data. This empirical generalization seems to have the qualifications for calling it an *empirical* law. However, I have chosen to call it "hypothesis" in this presentation. I cannot explain why Hypothesis 4 is plausible in terms of the principles and laws of rauding theory. It cannot be rationalistically derived from the principles of rauding theory.

Let me give you Hypothesis 4 before I ramble on too far. It is

$$\frac{1}{E} = \frac{1}{R} + i \qquad (17)$$

or

$$\frac{t}{T_c} = \frac{t}{T_p} + i \qquad (18)$$

You remember that R is the rate the passage is presented in thoughts per minute, so $1/R$ is the inverse, minutes per thought presented. Similarly, E is the efficiency at which the passage is comprehended in thoughts per minute, so $1/E$ is the inverse — minutes per thought comprehended. This quantified hypothesis, Hypothesis 4, stated that *the amount of time allowed per thought comprehended is equal to the amount of time allowed per thought presented plus a constant,* symbolized by i.

This lawful relationship will be especially difficult for me to explain to you, mainly because it is inherently complex, and there is no obvious reason why it should be true. I hope you will try to persevere, because it is the final link that allows the entire theory of rauding to be expressed quantitatively and succinctly.

Fran: I'll do my best to try to understand, although I have some doubt that I will ever need to understand rauding theory in this much detail.

Carver: I'm sure that some people will attempt to understand the unquantified aspects of the theory without bothering to try to understand the quantified aspects. However, if you ever want to test the theory or if you ever want to be able to evaluate evidence relevant to the theory, then you will need to understand how the entire theory is quantified.

When we finished the third hypothesis, earlier, we were halfway through the quantification of rauding theory. The third hypothesis, expressed in equation form, tells you what important factors the accuracy of comprehension of a passage depends upon when individuals are given less than enough time to operate the rauding process once on the passage. Hypothesis 4 tells you what the accuracy of comprehension of a passage depends upon when individuals are given more than enough time to operate the rauding process on the passage.

The most important thing you have to remember about Hypothesis 4 is that it only applies when a person has been given more than enough time to complete the passage at the rauding rate — presentation time exceeds rauding time or rate is less than rauding rate. In some circumstances, this means that a person has enough time to go back to the beginning of the passage and start executing the rauding process again and continue the execution of the rauding process until the end of the time period, t.

Equation 16 expressed Hypothesis 3 relating A and R when presentation time does not exceed rauding time; $t \leq t_r$. We can now rearrange Equation 17 so that it expresses Hypothesis 4 relating A and R.

If AR is substituted for E in Equation 17 and this equation is solved for A, we have

$$A = \frac{1/R}{1/R + i} \quad \text{when } R \leq R_r. \tag{19}$$

Although the fourth hypothesis may be quantitatively expressed as indicated in Equations 17 or 18, I prefer Equation 19 above. In this form, it is parallel to Equation 16, which also focuses upon accuracy, A, as a function of time per thought, $1/R$. Thus, I prefer Equation 16 as an expression of Hypothesis 3 and Equation 19 as an expression of Hypothesis 4. A verbal form of this fourth hypothesis is as follows: *The accuracy of comprehension of the passage is equal to the time per thought presented divided by the sum of the time per thought presented and the inefficiency constant, provided that the rate is less than or equal to the rauding rate.*

Fran: What is this *inefficiency constant?*

Carver: It is i, an index of the amount of inefficiency associated with the individual attempting to raud a passage. Without trying to explain why, for now, let me simply tell you that the inefficiency constant for a passage depends upon the rauding rate, R_r, and the rauding accuracy, A_r, as prescribed in this equation,

$$i = \frac{1}{R_r}\left(\frac{1}{A_r} - 1\right). \tag{20}$$

In the hypothetical example we worked with earlier, what was the value of R_r and A_r?

Fran: R_r was 20 sentences per minute and A_r was .80, so

$$i = \frac{1}{20} \left(\frac{1}{.80} - 1 \right) = 0.125.$$

Carver: Very good. In that example of yours can you now figure out what A would be if we kept increasing how much time you were allowed for rauding beyond the five minutes required to raud the passage once. You should substitute 6, 7, 8, 9, and 10 minutes into Equation 19 and solve for A.

Fran: First let me calculate the R values, using Equation 3 again, and invert these to get the $1/R$ values. Then, I'll calculate the A values.

$$R_6 = \frac{100}{6} = 16.7 \quad 1/R_6 = .06$$

$$R_7 = \frac{100}{7} = 14.3 \quad 1/R_7 = .07$$

$$R_8 = \frac{100}{8} = 12.5 \quad 1/R_8 = .08$$

$$R_9 = \frac{100}{9} = 11.1 \quad 1/R_9 = .09$$

$$R_{10} = \frac{100}{10} = 10.0 \quad 1/R_{10} = .10$$

$$A_6 = \frac{.06}{.06 + .0125} = .83$$

$$A_7 = \frac{.07}{.07 + .0125} = .85$$

$$A_8 = \frac{.08}{.08 + .0125} = .87$$

$$A_9 = \frac{.09}{.09 + .0125} = .88$$

$$A_{10} = \frac{.10}{.10 + .0125} = .89$$

Carver: All right. Let's plot these values of A on a graph — A_6, A_7, A_8, A_9, A_{10} — together with the A values for the first five time intervals — A_1, A_2, A_3, A_4, A_5 — as a function of the time variable, $1/R$. Look at Figure 2. Notice that rauding theory now claims that the proportion of this hypothetical passage that you will understand will increase from zero in a linear manner, $A = 16(1/R)$, up until you are allowed enough time to finish the

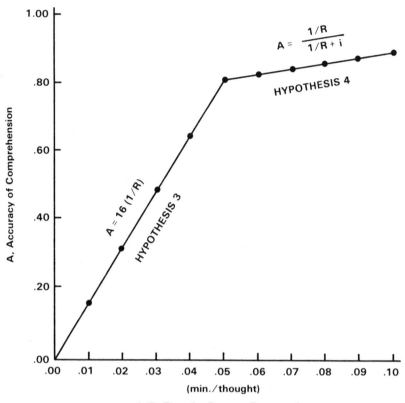

Figure 2.

rauding process once. The point where you complete the rauding process on the passage is when $t = 5$ minutes and $1/R = .05$ minutes per thought. From this point on, the accuracy of passage comprehension will keep on increasing as you are allowed more time, but it will no longer be in a perfectly linear manner. The curve in Figure 2 appears to be perfectly linear, but it is not.

It should not escape your notice that we were able to calculate or predict how much of the passage you would comprehend after varying amounts of time allowed, given only a knowledge of your rauding rate, plus your rauding accuracy for this passage, or passages of similar levels of rauding difficulty.

Fran: It would be impressive if from rauding theory you could accurately predict how much of a passage I would comprehend after various amounts of time spent reading. You would need to know my rauding rate in advance ($R_r = ?$), and you also would need to know enough about me and the passage to be able to estimate what my accuracy of comprehension would be at the point when I finished rauding the passage once ($A_r = ?$).

Carver: This is true. Now, I'd like to explain to you how one may go about estimating or measuring a person's R_r and A_r values.

Fran: Wait a minute! I'm not through with this topic yet. I would like for you to talk some more about i, the inefficiency index. What is it, and why does it equal what you said it did?

Carver: I guess I'm not through with the topic either because I haven't gotten to the empirical data yet. I'll postpone, for now, explaining about measuring a person's A_r and R_r. Instead, let's go back and look at these same data that you have just calculated, but instead of looking at the relationship between A and $1/R$, let's look at $1/E$ versus $1/R$. $1/E$ is the opposite of efficiency; a high value of $1/E$ would be high inefficiency and a low value of $1/E$ would be low inefficiency. When we take a look at $1/E$ versus $1/R$ we are looking at what happens to the inefficiency of passage comprehension as the presentation time is increased.

To look at the relationship between $1/E$ and $1/R$, I'm going to ask you to calculate the $1/E$ values that go with each of the $1/R$ values we worked with earlier.

Fran:

$$\frac{1}{E_1} = \frac{1}{A_1 R_1} = \frac{1}{(.16)(100)} = .0625$$

$$\frac{1}{E_2} = \frac{1}{A_2 R_2} = \frac{1}{(.32)(50)} = .0625$$

$$\frac{1}{E_3} = \frac{1}{A_3 R_3} = \frac{1}{(.48)(33.3)} = .0625$$

$$\frac{1}{E_4} = \frac{1}{A_4 R_4} = \frac{1}{(.64)(25)} = .0625$$

$$\frac{1}{E_5} = \frac{1}{A_5 R_5} = \frac{1}{(.80)(20)} = .0625$$

$$\frac{1}{E_6} = \frac{1}{A_6 R_6} = \frac{1}{(.83)(16.7)} = .0721$$

$$\frac{1}{E_7} = \frac{1}{A_7 R_7} = \frac{1}{(.85)(14.3)} = .0823$$

$$\frac{1}{E_8} = \frac{1}{A_8 R_8} = \frac{1}{(.87)(12.5)} = .0920$$

$$\frac{1}{E_9} = \frac{1}{A_9 R_9} = \frac{1}{(.88)(11.1)} = .1024$$

$$\frac{1}{E_{10}} = \frac{1}{A_{10} R_{10}} = \frac{1}{(89)(10)} = .1124$$

Carver: I'll plot these 10 $1/E$ values that you have calculated as a function of their corresponding $1/R$ values in Figure 3. Notice that on this graph both curves are straight lines. One curve is represented by the equation $1/E = .0625$ and the other by $1/E = 1/R + .0125$.

When short amounts of presentation time are allowed — $t \leq 5$ or $1/R \leq .05$ — then the amount of inefficiency is a constant at .0625. This is saying that when you have control over the rate at which you operate your rauding process, the overall amount of passage inefficiency, $1/E$ or $1/AR$, stays constant no matter how much time you are allowed on the passage. Then, at the five-

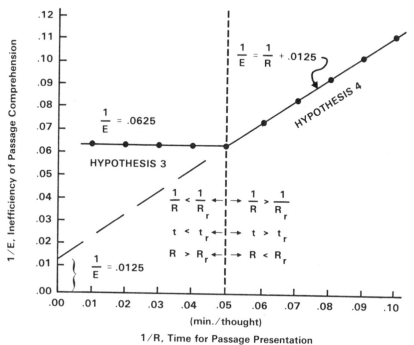

Figure 3.

minute mark where $1/R = .05$, inefficiency starts increasing, and it increases in a linear manner. The straight line that describes this relationship has a slope of 1.00 and an intercept that is symbolized by i; $i = .0125$ is the point where the straight line,

$$\frac{1}{E} = \frac{1}{R} + .0125,$$

crosses the y-axis or the value of $1/E$ when $1/R = 0$. If you can find a situation where it is reasonable to infer that a person has been given more than enough time to finish rauding a passage once, we can then estimate, or measure, A and R. These values allow us to plot our calculated values of $1/E$ and $1/R$, and we should then find a linear relationship. The linear relationship is the most we should expect to find empirically, since the slope of the empirical line may not be 1.00 and the intercept may not be zero for the same scaling reasons we discussed earlier.

Fran: I did not understand this last point.

Carver: I'll try to say it another way. If rauding theory is sound, we should find empirical support for the following sub-hypothesis derived from the fourth hypothesis:

$$\frac{1}{E} = b\frac{1}{R} + a. \tag{21}$$

We should find that a measure of inefficiency, $1/E$, increases linearly with increases in the time allowed for rauding a passage, $1/R$. Notice that if we did not have rescaling problems, then b would equal 1.00 and a would equal i, giving us Equation 17. However, if we do have scaling problems, as we would expect in the real world, then the slope of this line will not be 1.00, and the intercept will not equal i. I will be able to explain this better later when we deal with rescaling again, so I'll ask you to let me go on without your having a completely satisfying explanation of these ideas.

The fourth hypothesis was developed from empirical data collected for another purpose, so it is crucial to determine whether there is independently collected data that support this part of the theory. It is especially important in this instance, since there are no principles, laws, or supporting rationale that explain why this hypothesis should hold as it does.

Fran: Before you start telling me about the empirical data that support this part of rauding theory, let me remind you that you have not told me where you got the equation for calculating i.

Carver: Sorry about that! As I said before, we simply let i stand for the intercept of the straight line when $1/E$ was plotted as a function of $1/R$, that is,

$$\frac{1}{E} = \frac{1}{R} + i. \tag{22}$$

Then we solve the equation for i,

$$i = \frac{1}{E} - \frac{1}{R} \tag{23}$$

and substitute AR for E as follows:

$$i = \frac{1}{AR} - \frac{1}{R}. \tag{24}$$

Then we factor out $1/R$ to get

$$i = \frac{1}{R}\left(\frac{1}{A} - 1\right). \tag{25}$$

This equation holds at the point where $t = t_r$. At this point, $R = R_r$. When the rate, R, is R_r then the accuracy, A, must be A_r. Therefore, substituting R_r and A_r for R and A in Equation 25 gives you Equation 20,

$$i = \frac{1}{R_r}\left(\frac{1}{A_r} - 1\right).$$

Since i stays constant, whatever value we find for it when $R = R_r$ and $A = A_r$ will remain true for the rest of the curve where $R < R_r$ and $A > A_r$.

Fran: That seems complex. I'm confident that I could raud it if I took the time to study it first. I'd rather go on now and worry about rauding it later. I think I'm ready for your introduction of the data that is relevant to situations where presentation time exceeds rauding time.

Carver: Do you remember my description of Study II where 102 college students were asked to read and aud Grade 5, 8, 11, and 14 passages at 10 different rates?

Fran: That was the study where the passages were presented orally using time-compressed speech and visually using motion picture film, wasn't it?

Carver: Right. For those rates where it was reasonable to assume that the students were given more than enough time to execute the rauding process on the passage, the correlation between $1/E$ values and the $1/R$ values was perfect.

Fran: What?

Carver: The correlation coefficient was used as a measure of how well a straight line fit the data — how well Equation 21 fit the data. There were eight situations where this correlation could be computed; there were four different levels of passage difficulty, and at each of these four levels there were both auding data and reading data. For the data in these eight situations where it was reasonable to assume that the individuals had more than enough time to operate the rauding process, a correlation was computed between the estimates of $1/E$ and $1/R$. Six of the eight correlations were 1.00 and two were .99. Thus, Study II provides strong support for the hypothesis expressed in Equation 21 that the relationship between $1/E$ and $1/R$ is linear as long as $R \leq R$, or $1/R \geq 1/R_r$, or $t \geq t_r$. In Study II, there were also data which on a rational basis did not appear to need to be rescaled, and for these data the slopes of these straight lines was almost perfect; there were three slopes (b values in Equation 21) that were 1.0, three that were .9, and two were 1.1. Thus, the fourth hypothesis that

$$\frac{1}{E} = \frac{1}{R} + i \qquad \text{from Equation (17),}$$

has support for the slope of this line being 1.0, and these data seem to provide strong support for this part of rauding theory.

Before I go on to describe Study III and the empirical support it provides for Hypothesis 4, let me digress and say a few more words about Study II and Hypothesis 3.

Rauding theory has something quantitative to say about the accuracy of comprehension of a passage in Hypothesis 3 as long as the *average rate* that the passage is presented is greater than the rauding rate. These are situations in which the individual has control over the rauding process rate. In these situations, presentation time for a passage is what is being manipulated not the *actual rate* at which the words are presented. The actual rate may be manipulated by motion picture film or by time-compressed speech, as was mentioned earlier in connection with Study II. When actual rate is being manipulated, this means that an attempt is being made to manipulate the rauding process rate. When average rate is being manipulated by controlling the length of time that a passage is presented, the individuals are free to operate their rauding process at their own rauding rate.

When the actual rate that the passage is presented does, in fact, exceed the rauding rate, R_r, then Hypothesis 3 would not be purported to be valid. Hypothesis 3 is only purported to be valid when presentation time, t, is being manipulated so that individuals are free to operate their rauding process at their rauding rate. In contrast to Hypothesis 3, Hypothesis 4 is purported to be valid under both of these passage presentation conditions — when actual rate *or* presentation time are being manipulated. Now I'm going to put Table I on the chalkboard. This table summarizes and organizes what I have been saying.

The first row in Table I is concerned with situations where rate is being directly manipulated, as it was in Study II using motion picture film and time-compressed speech. As I said earlier, in these situations R is therefore the actual rate, not an average rate. Notice that Hypothesis 3 is not purported to be valid under these conditions, whereas Hypothesis 4 is purported to be valid.

The next row in the table is concerned with situations in which the time that a passage is presented is manipulated, *not* actual rate. In these situations, R is an average rate, not an actual rate. Under this type of passage presentation condition both Hypoth-

TABLE I

Passage Presentation Condition	Qualifying Note	Hypothesis Number	Is Hypothesis Purported to Be Valid?
Manipulate R, rate, e.g. Study II	R is therefore actual rate, not average rate.	3	NO
		4	YES
Manipulate t, presentation time, e.g. Study III	R is therefore average rate, not actual rate.	3	YES
		4	YES

TABLE II

Hypothesis Number	Formula Statement	Valid When	Qualification Notes
3	$A = A_r R_r \dfrac{1}{R}$	$t \leq t_r$ $R \geq R_r$ $\dfrac{1}{R} \leq \dfrac{1}{R_r}$	Hypothesis 3 is purported to be valid only when t, but not R, is manipulated so that R is average rate *not* actual rate.
4	$A = \dfrac{1/R}{1/R + i}$	$t \geq t_r$ $R \leq R_r$ $\dfrac{1}{R} \geq \dfrac{1}{R_r}$	Hypothesis 4 is purported to be valid when either t *or* R is manipulated so R may be either average rate or actual rate.

esis 3 and Hypothesis 4 are purported to be valid. Study III, which I keep promising to describe to you, will provide an example for you of an experimental situation in which presentation time is being manipulated so that R is an average rate, not an actual rate.

Fran: I keep forgetting what Hypothesis 3 and Hypothesis 4 are while I'm trying to follow what you are saying.

Carver: Let me put another table on the chalkboard for you; it should help you with that problem.

Table II summarizes for you what each hypothesis is in formula form, gives the conditions under which it is valid, and explains again how manipulating time or rate qualifies what R means for Hypothesis 3. I'll give you some time to study Table II.

Fran: I can understand that it makes a difference whether actual rate or average rate is being manipulated, but I'm not sure I understand *why* this is the case.

Carver: Hypothesis 3 is based on the idea that the rauding process will operate at the rauding rate whenever individuals are free to choose their own rate. Whenever presentation time is what is being manipulated, then individuals are allowed to choose their own rate, so it is reasonable to advance Hypothesis 3 in these situations. However, if the actual rate is being manipulated, then the individual is not free to operate the rauding process at the rauding rate, so there is no reason to contend that Hypothesis 3 is valid.

Fran: I understand that, but why is Hypothesis 4 purported to be valid both when presentation time is being manipulated and also actual rate is being manipulated.

Carver: You must remember that Hypothesis 4 was not derived from the theory but was an empirical generalization. There was no restriction placed upon the generalization when it was developed from the data, and the data that have been collected seem to support Hypothesis 4 when presentation time or actual rate have been manipulated. In short, I cannot explain why Hypothesis 4 holds when actual rate is being manipulated; I can only tell you that this is the way it is, or appears to be.

Fran: This is unsettling from a rationalistic standpoint. I guess I cannot complain too much, however, since I have always been more of an empiricist than a rationalist anyway.

Carver: I'd like to elaborate upon these ideas that we have been talking about by switching to an efficiency context. I'm now going to talk about the effect of manipulating t and R upon E and $1/E$.

Rauding theory holds that people who are forced to read or aud at a rate that is beyond their rauding rate will not be able to understand or comprehend the thoughts. So, when actual rate is manipulated to a point where it is higher than R_r, then E should drop and $1/E$, or inefficiency, should increase dramatically. In Figure 3, average rate was being manipulated, not actual rate. Therefore, you do not see this dramatic increase in $1/E$ when $1/R < 1/R_r$. Instead, you see $1/E$ being constant at .0625. As long as the individuals are allowed to proceed at their own rauding rate, the amount of passage inefficiency will be constant.

Whenever you manipulate actual rate and force a person to go faster than his/her rauding rate, either when auding or when reading, then he/she should not comprehend thoughts well at all. This is the threshold aspect of rauding rate. Rauding rate is not only supposed to be a constant type of rate and an optimal type of rate, but it should also have the properties of a threshold rate when actual R is manipulated. Study II contains data that provide support for the threshold aspect of rauding rate because inefficiency increased dramatically when $1/R$ was lower than $1/R_r$.

Fran: I'm not rauding!

Carver: Okay. I'll elaborate some more upon this threshold idea. Let's begin with a situation where actual rate is less than the rauding rate, or the time per thought presented is greater than the amount of time per thought required at the rauding rate, $1/R > 1/R_r$. This should be highly inefficient because you have more time than you need to raud. Then, if you decrease the time per thought presented by increasing actual rate so that $1/R$ decreases, then inefficiency should decrease in accordance with Hypothesis 4 and depicted in Figure 3. This is expected from rauding theory because it is very inefficient to give people more time than they need to operate the rauding process. As the actual rate is increased so that $1/R$ gets closer to $1/R_r$, the amount of inefficiency decreases. The decrease should be steady and follow the straight line I talked about earlier and depicted as $1/E = 1/R + .0125$ in Figure 9. When the actual rate is increased so that $1/R$ is exactly equal to $1/R_r$, then inefficiency is at a minimum; this is the same as saying that efficiency is at a maximum. If the actual rate is further increased beyond R_r, so that $1/R < 1/R_r$, then there should be an increase in inefficiency. However this increase in inefficiency should not be gradual; rather, there should be a dramatic increase in inefficiency that reflects a threshold effect. Indeed, the data in Study II provide strong support for the existence of this threshold increase in $1/E$ when $1/R$ is decreased below $1/R_r$. These data in Study II are not relevant to Hypothesis 3 because actual rate instead of average rate is being manipulated. However, these data do support the threshold nature of the rauding rate.

Taken together, Study I and Study II provide excellent empirical support for the existence of rauding rate as an entity that has the property of being constant across passages of varying levels of difficulty, has the property of being associated with maximum efficiency, and has the property of being a threshold rate beyond which inefficiency increases dramatically. Thus, Study I and Study II support the principles and laws of rauding theory that are based upon the existence of a rauding rate for each person, which is relatively constant, is optimal, and is a threshold rate.

Fran: You have convinced me that Study I and Study II are extremely important in terms of providing an empirical under-pinning for rauding theory. But you still have not gotten to Study III. What is in it that is relevant to Hypothesis 4?

Carver: I'm now ready to answer that question. The same 102 college students who took part in Study II also took part in Study III. These students were given passages to read for varying lengths of time. Average rate, measured in standard length words per minute, varied from 62.5 Wpm to 100,000 Wpm. It is important to understand that presentation time was the variable that was manipulated in Study III, not actual rate. Remember, actual rate was manipulated in Study II by varying the speed at which the words in the passages were presented via motion picture film or time-compressed speech. In Study III, only read-ing was involved, not auding, and the time that the entire pas-sage was presented was varied to produce average rates between 62.5 and 100,000 Wpm. So, the R values and $1/R$ values in Study III were average rates, not actual manipulated rates as they were in Study II. The individuals were free to operate their rauding process on a passage at a rate of their own choosing in Study III. In Study III, both Hypothesis 3 and Hypothesis 4 may be tested because both are purported to be valid.

The passages in Study III were selected to represent Grade 10 difficulty, so most of these college students should have been able to raud this level of material difficulty. There were several measures used, and these measures combined with the instruc-tions were designed to produce different purposes for reading. However, the similarity of the pattern of results between pur-pose conditions suggested that the subjects probably attempted to raud under all of the purpose conditions. This result may be interpreted as providing additional support for the First Law of Rauding.

Altogether, there were four different measurement tech-niques employed in Study III to estimate an individual's accura-cy of passage comprehension, A. As in Study II, one measure was subjective ratings by the individuals regarding what percent of the sentences in each passage they thought they had understood. There were three objective measures — Missing Verbs Test, Best Titles Test, and Sentences-Halves Test — which also provided an accuracy score for each passage at each rate for each individual. After the objective measures were rescaled — to be explained later — it was found that all four measures produced almost exactly the same estimates of A. This result suggested that rauding theory provides valid estimates of A under a variety of methods for estimating A.

It was possible in this study to use Equations 16 and 19 from Hypothesis 3 and Hypothesis 4 to produce theoretically predicted values for A at each rate. The R_r and A_r values used in these equations were based upon group averages — rauding rate (305 Wpm) and rauding accuracy (.78).

Fran: Where did these values come from?

Carver: I will explain how I got them later, when I talk about the details of measurement. I'll do that after I finish giving you this overview of the data that support the hypothesis of rauding theory. When you raud the research report of the Study III data, these measurement details will be explained thoroughly. For now, please accept that there are empirical procedures for estimating R_r and A_r.

Fran: Okay, I'll wait.

Carver: Now, for this group of 102 students their average estimated R_r value was 18.3 thoughts per minute, and their average estimated A_r value was .78. When these values are substituted in Equation 16 and Equation 19, expected or predicted value of A can be obtained for each value of $1/R$. It was found that those rates *higher* than 1000 Wpm tended to produce zero estimates for A. For those rates *lower* than 1000 Wpm the theoretically predicted values of A were extremely close to the empirically measured values — the average of the prediction errors was only about 3.5 percentage points.

Fran: I assume the empirical estimates of A came from your four comprehension measures in the experiment, but tell me again how you got the theoretically predicted values of A.

Carver: Again, I used Equations 16 and 19. Estimates of R_r and A_r were substituted into these equations, along with the various $1/R$ values, and then A was solved for. The average difference between the twenty empirical values of A and their corresponding theoretically predicted values was only about three percentage points, as I said earlier. This means that rauding theory predicted how much of these passages this group would comprehend within about 3 percent, on the average. For this theory to be able to predict the percent of each passage that this group would comprehend at various average rates, and do it relatively accurately, is no small feat. To my knowledge, there is no existing competitor to rauding theory. There is no way to compare rauding theory with another theory on the basis of the degree of prediction error, because I know of no other theory that would make a prediction regarding what proportion of a passage individuals would comprehend. Yet, it is possible to evaluate rauding theory on an absolute basis, and on this basis a 3 percent average error in predictions made from the two quantified hypotheses of the theory seems impressive to me.

Fran: Equation 16 expresses Hypothesis 3, and Equation 19 expresses Hypothesis 4, so you are contending that these data from Study III provide support for Hypothesis 3 as well as for Hypothesis 4.

Carver: Exactly. I think that if you examine Study III closely you will see that it provides strong support for rauding theory in general. In particular, it provides strong support for the theorized relationships among A, R, E, R_r, A_r, and t, when t is less than, equal to, and greater than t_r. In turn, these data provide indirect support for all Three Laws of Rauding Theory.

Fran: Again, I take what you have told me as being impressive and certainly worthy of further study on my part. But, I think I need to raud the research reports themselves to adequately weigh the evidence.

Carver: Once you attempt to raud Studies I, II, and III, you will be knee-deep into the practicalities of measurement. You will see how the empirical indicators of T_c, T_p, t, A, R, E, R_r, and E_r are derived. You will also see how measures of the rauding ability of the individual and the rauding difficulty of the passage are derived. The next thing I'm going to do is talk about these measurement problems and my suggested solutions. Then, when I am through with that, I'm going to take a long break — long enough for you to raud the research reports that contain the supporting empirical data. When we resume, I'll assume you know enough about rauding theory and its supporting data to be able to criticize it yourself, evaluate others' criticisms of it, and discuss its implications.

Chapter 8

HOW ARE THE IMPORTANT VARIABLES IN RAUDING THEORY MEASURED?

Carver: Philosophers of science have written extensively about how theory gets tested via empirical procedures. These discussions usually involve such terms as correspondence rules, operational definitions, coordinating definitions, rules of interpretation, semantical rules, and epistemic correlations. Traditionally, in education and psychology the terminology "operational definition" has been used most often in connection with measurement problems and their solutions. Until now I have tried to explain to you the ideas underlying rauding theory without getting deeply involved in operational definitions. We must now come to grips with the rationale underlying measurement of the important variables in rauding theory.

Fran: Good. I have never understood all the interconnections you have made among sentences, words, syllables, standard length words, and standard length sentences.

Carver: Many other people have had this same problem. Let me try to organize for you what I want to tell you about measurement. Altogether, there will be seven topics that I must cover. The first pair of topics will deal with A and R, i.e. measuring the accuracy of passage comprehension, Topic 1, and the rate of passage presentation, Topic 2. Then, I'll talk about A_r and R_r, i.e. rauding accuracy, Topic 3, and rauding rate, Topic 4. The third pair of topics will deal with the rauding ability of the individual, Topic 5, and the rauding difficulty of the passage, Topic 6. Finally, I will try to explain the most difficult topic of all, the rauding rescaling procedure that I have alluded to before, Topic 7.

Before I get into the details of these topics, let's review and reinforce some of the facets of rauding. Take a look at what I'm going to put on the chalkboard for you.

The writer has ideas or thoughts that he/she wants to express

102

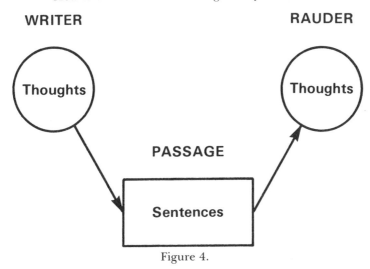

Figure 4.

and communicate to others. Therefore, the writer puts these thoughts into words and organizes them in the form of interconnected sentences, called a passage. The *rauder* desires to understand these thoughts of the writer, so the rauder attempts to understand each of the writer's sentences because this is the most effective way of making sure this communication of thoughts takes place. Rauding occurs when the thoughts that the writer intended to communicate are, in fact, communicated to the rauder via the understanding of each consecutive sentence in a passage.

Rauding theory has chosen to focus upon the thought as a primary theoretical unit just as certain physical theories have often chosen to focus upon the atom. However, when the time arrives for drawing up the corresponding rules between the theory and the real world, the importance of the sentence as a unit looms large.

As mentioned earlier, the sentence is an important unit in the rauding process because it was theorized that the rauding process operates by attempting to comprehend the complete thought contained in each consecutive sentence in a passage. The sentence will also be an important unit for estimating the accuracy of comprehension because it will be theorized that the proportion of sentences in a passage that was comprehended provides a good estimate of the proportion of thoughts comprehended.

It should not come as a surprise to you that the sentence is involved in the empirical techniques I use to measure the rate at which a passage is presented and the accuracy with which it is comprehended. What probably comes as a surprise is how syllables, letters, spaces, standard length words, and standard length sentences get involved. My task is to describe to you how the comprehension of thoughts in a passage is operationally defined and measured by using units other than thoughts.

Fran: It seems to me that you have articulated the problem well. I'm looking forward to the solution, and I am not extremely optimistic that you will be able to convince me that your solution is sound.

Carver: Your pessimism presents quite a challenge. It will help me if we use symbols to designate certain variables. T_p is more associated with the number of thoughts in the head of the writer, and T_c is more associated with the number of the author's thoughts that made it all the way to the head of the rauder. If we let the acutal number of sentences in the passage be symbolized by s_p and the actual number of sentences the rauder understood be symbolized by s_c, then the communication process can be represented as

$$T_p \longrightarrow s_p \longrightarrow s_c \longrightarrow T_c.$$

The progression of the arrows indicates the thoughts flowing from the author to the articulated sentences and then to the reader via the comprehension of these sentences.

Topic 1 – Estimating A

With this background, we are now ready to begin the first topic, various ways of estimating the accuracy of passage comprehension. Remember that

$$A = \frac{T_c}{T_p}, \qquad \text{from Equation (2).}$$

It does not seem like a big leap to infer that the proportion of thoughts understood, T_c/T_p, is approximately equal to the proportion of sentences understood, that is,

$$\frac{T_c}{T_p} \cong \frac{s_c}{s_p}. \tag{26}$$

(Notice that the symbol $\cong$ is used to designate "approximately equal.") Thus, if we have some way of estimating the proportion of sentences understood s_c/s_p, we will have a reasonable empirical measure of the proportion of thoughts understood, T_c/T_p.

It will help me explain things more precisely if I interrupt myself and develop more precise symbols to use. Let me put a bar(-) over a variable to indicate that values of the variable have been estimated by an empirical measurement technique. For example, if I had given a test to estimate the accuracy of comprehension, I could designate the variable that results as $\bar{A}$. If I estimate the rate that the passage was presented by using some technique that involved counting letter spaces and dividing by the time involved, then I could designate the variable that results as $\bar{R}$. In my discussions of accuracy, A, I will find it necessary to discriminate between empirical estimates that are possibly biased and in need of rescaling as compared to empirical estimates that are considered to be unbiased. I will use a tilde ($\tilde{}$) on top of A, $\tilde{A}$, to designate an empirical estimate of A that is considered to be unbiased. Rescaling $\bar{A}$ values produces $\tilde{A}$ values. Other techniques may be considered as providing $\tilde{A}$ values without rescaling. For example, using these symbol conventions, we can say that

$$\bar{A} = \frac{s_c}{s_p}. \tag{27}$$

This means that dividing a measure of the number of sentences comprehended by a measure of the number of sentences presented produces a type of $\bar{A}$ value of comprehension, so we will designate it as $\bar{A}$.

Fran: What do you mean by "biased" and "unbiased"?

Carver: In this situation, an unbiased measure is one that does not systematically overestimate or underestimate A values. For example, a college student taking a cloze test on an extremely difficult passage may get 30 percent of the cloze blanks correct, $\bar{A}$ = .30. However, A may actually be .00 in this situation because the student may have comprehended 0 percent of the thoughts in the passage. The cloze measure is likely to produce a systematically biased estimate of A. However, this does not mean that the cloze test is necessarily invalid. It may produce $\bar{A}$ values that correlate highly with A values; for example, when the cloze score is low, then A is also low, and when the cloze score is high, then A is also high. Rescaling cloze scores may produce valid $\bar{A}$ values. Some $\bar{A}$ measures may be assumed to produce valid $\tilde{A}$ values without rescaling, such as the percent of sentences comprehended, mentioned earlier. In some cases, it may be reasonable to assume that judgments of A by the subjects themselves produce $\bar{A}$ values that are also valid as $\tilde{A}$ values.

Fran: I am not rauding what you are saying.

Carver: Let me give you some examples. In Study II, there were a number of ways of estimating A via s_c/s_p; there were a number of empirical techniques for determining $\tilde{A}$. One way was to let the individuals make their own judgments of s_c/s_p — each person was asked to estimate the percentage of the sentences in a passage that he/she understood. For example, if there were eight sentences in a passage and it was an individual's opinion that he/she understood two of them, then the individual would report a 25 percent figure. I would then divide these percents by 100 to convert them to the proportions that are the units of A. This technique for providing $\bar{A}$ may be considered as unbiased so it may also be regarded as providing $\tilde{A}$ values. Another technique for estimating A was to use a paraphrase multiple-choice question on each sentence in a passage. The number of questions answered correctly would be an indicator of s_c and the total number of questions in the passage would be an indicator of s_p. However, this estimation technique for providing $\bar{A}$ values is not likely to provide unbiased estimates of A, so it would not be regarded as also providing $\tilde{A}$ values. Let me note parenthetically that this particular measure of A was actually not the number of questions answered correctly divided by the total number of questions, because a correction for guessing was applied to the number of questions answered correctly; this is simply a standard correction procedure used with multiple-choice questions and has no important bearing upon the present discussion.

Fran: So, $\bar{A}$ is always an empirical estimate of A that comes from some measure of the proportion of sentences that were understood.

Carver: Not necessarily. Remember the cloze technique I mentioned earlier. There are other techniques that reflect the proportion of the passage that was comprehended without any direct involvement of sentences. For example, in Study II, an objective type of measure was used that involved the deletion of all but the first letters of certain words, and the task was to determine which ones of these skeleton words had been changed from the original passage. This is called the reading-storage technique, and it simply provides another way of estimating the proportion of thoughts in the passage that had been comprehended. Thus, this technique provided $\bar{A}$ values not based upon s_c/s_p. The rationale underlying the validity of this technique is that it is a correlate of T_c/T_p; it probably produces valid $\bar{A}$ values but probably does not provide valid $\tilde{A}$ values.

It is important that you understand these distinctions before you raud Study II. Before many of the quantitative hypotheses of rauding theory can be expected to work — be appropriately tested — the values used for A must be on a scale that goes from .00 to 1.00; .00 when none of the sentences in the passage were comprehended and 1.00 when all of the sentences 100 percent were comprehended. Sometimes measures of $\bar{A}$ should be rescaled to provide valid $\tilde{A}$ values. Other times, it seems reasonable to assume that the $\bar{A}$ values provide valid $\tilde{A}$ values without rescaling.

Fran: Does this mean that it is possible to use any technique to measure $\bar{A}$ and as long as it can be rescaled into $\tilde{A}$ values, it will likely be a valid estimate of A?

Carver: That is almost right. I have used a variety of empirical techniques, and I have been impressed that all have provided data that supported rauding theory when they were rescaled.

Fran: And, you are going to explain rescaling, later.

Carver: Right. I will describe the rauding rescaling procedure last, Topic 7. For now, let me describe a relatively simple rescaling technique that can be and has been used. Do you recall that I told you that one way of estimating A was to ask students to make judgments about s_c/s_p after they finished a passage?

Fran: Yes. You said you asked them to rate the percent of the sentences they understood, didn't you?

Carver: Right. This subjective technique for getting $\bar{A}$ values also seemed to provide especially good $\tilde{A}$ values. The results from the other techniques — the objective techniques — were found to be highly correlated with these subjective judgments so the regression equation associated with the correlation coefficient was used to rescale. The regression equation allows you to obtain a predicted subjective value for each objective value, so each objective value was rescaled to provide predicted subjective values. Since the subjective values were considered to provide $\tilde{A}$ values, this has the effect of transforming the $\bar{A}$ values from the objective measures into $\tilde{A}$ values, and thereupon to provide eligible values to use to test hypotheses about A.

You should understand that there is nothing unreasonable or highly questionable about this procedure, since the rescaled values are simply linear transforms; it is analogous to transforming raw scores to z scores or z scores to T scores so that nothing of substance has changed. Stated differently, you must understand that this rescaling does not automatically provide empirical results that support rauding theory. Instead, it simply makes these data more appropriate for testing rauding theory.

Before we took off on this tangent about rescaling, I had just mentioned that I had found a variety of measurement techniques that had supported rauding theory when rescaled. Let me list the names of the measurement technqiues that were used in Studies II and III: understanding judgments, reading-storage tests, paraphrase tests, missing verbs tests, best titles tests, and sentence-halves tests.

Of course, if you use a measure of passage comprehension that does not give representative coverage to all parts of the passages or all sentences in a passage, then you are apt to run into trouble if you think you are going to use the measure to test rauding theory. For example, if your measure is called "the main idea test" and it reflects primarily what is contained in the first sentence or first part of the passage, then scores on this test probably would not be appropriate for testing rauding theory. This is because these scores probably would not provide good $\bar{A}$

values because they could not be rescaled to provide valid $\tilde{A}$ values. As long as the empirical measurement technique provides scores that are representative of the comprehension of all the sentences in a passage, then it can probably be rescaled and thereupon be appropriate for testing rauding theory. Thus, the theory is not very restrictive in terms of the type of measurement techniques that may be created to test its quantitative hypotheses, as long as the measurement technique provides a representative sample of all parts of a passage. Do you have any questions about empirical techniques for estimating A, before we move on to the next topic, R?

Fran: No, except I am still a little puzzled about how you handle those situations in which people can score above zero or above chance on tests and still not have comprehended any of the sentences in the passage.

Carver: That is exactly the rescaling problem that I plan to cover when I describe the rauding rescaling procedure in Topic 7. Let's move on to empirical techniques for estimating the rate of passage presentation, my second topic.

Topic 2 – Estimating **R**

Carver: It would be straightforward if we simply measured the rate at which a passage was presented by dividing the number of sentences in the passage, s_p, by the presentation time, t. This would be possible, and indeed it would not be wrong. However, it would not be right either. The rauding process operates upon sentences as comparable chunks from a comprehension standpoint, but it does not operate upon sentences as comparable chunks from a rate standpoint. As I discussed toward the beginning, the words are said to oneself, internally articulated, at a rate that allows T_c/t to be maximized, but the purest measure of rate that capitalized upon its constancy would involve syllables. However, syllables are notoriously difficult to count reliably. Letters and spaces are also tedious to count but even untrained or unskilled workers can count them relatively reliably — even a computer can do it.

A ruler can often be used to count since letterspaces typed by most typewriters are a direct function of line length in inches or centimeters. Since the number of letters and spaces in a passage is highly correlated with the number of syllables in a passage, then we should not lose much substance or accuracy by choosing to count letters and spaces in a passage rather than syllables. To make letters and spaces more meaningful, I decided to create a standard length word by dividing the total number of letters and spaces by 6. This convention is also used in typing instruction to measure typing rate in words per minute. Thus, six letter spaces is by definition a standard length word. I am telling you this to review what I talked about earlier.

Now let me give you an example of how you determine rate in standard length words per minute. Suppose you read the following sentence in one second:

The quick brown fox said to the brown cow, "How now?"

Starting with the first letter and counting all of the letters in the words, the spaces between words, and the punctuation, there are a total of fifty-three letter spaces in the sentence above. There is also an arbitrary rule that two spaces will be counted at the end of each sentence just as if there were another sentence following it. Thus, to get the number of standard length words in this sentence we would divide 55 by 6 to get 9.17 standard length words per second, or by multiplying this by 60, we get 550 standard length words per minute, 550 Wpm. Since there are actually 11 words in the sentence, the traditional rate would be 11 words per second or 660 words per minute, 660 wpm.

One major problem with measuring rate in syllables per minute or standard length words per minute is that neither one fits in very well with our accent upon the thought or the sentence as a unit. For example, if we measured A and found it to be .70 and we measured R and found it to be 400 Wpm, then E would be .70 × 400 or 280 Wpm. It sounds very strange to say that the efficiency with which an individual comprehended a passage was 280 Wpm, or that 280 words were being comprehended each minute. In an effort to make the theory more meaningful, rate will be measured alternately in *standard length sentences.* Based upon some average sentence length data that I had access to years ago, I decided to let 100 letterspaces be a standard

length sentence, or a standard length thought. Since there are 6
letter spaces per standard length word, this means that there will
be 100/6 or 16.7 standard length words per each standard length
sentence.

In the example above, there are 55/100 or .55 standard length
sentences, and when read in one second this results in a rate of
33 standard length *sentences per minute*, 33 Spm. When I want to
lean toward the empirical side, I will say 33 Spm; when I want to
lean toward the theoretical side I will say 33 standard length
thoughts per minute or say that I have estimated the rate to be 33
thoughts per min. By measuring rate in sentences per minute,
using a standard length sentence, we get an estimate of efficiency from $E = AR$ that is also in sentences per minute; $E = (.70)$
(33) or 23.1 Spm. It seems to make more sense to say that an
individual's efficiency was 23.1 Spm or the individual was comprehending sentences at a rate of 23.1 every minute as opposed
to saying that the individual was comprehending 280 words each
minute.

By measuring rate in standard length sentences per minute
and by measuring accuracy in terms of the proportion of actual
sentences understood, we seem to have some inconsistencies.
However, the inconsistencies are more apparent than real. In
effect, we are saying that the number of words in a passage (w_p) is
a correlate of the number of thoughts in a passage, T_p, that is

$$T_p = f(w_p), \tag{28}$$

but that the number of standard length words in a passage (W_p)
is also a correlate of T_p, that is

$$T_p = f(W_p). \tag{29}$$

Furthermore, it seems reasonable to assume that W_p is a *higher*
correlate of T_p than w_p.

Fran: I think I'm lost. Can you spell this out another way?

Carver: I'm saying that it seems reasonable to assume that for
most of the passages that exist in the real world, those that have
more words contain more thoughts and those that contain less
words contain less thoughts. This is what I meant when I said
that the number of thoughts in a passage was a function of, or a

correlate of, the number of words in the passage. Then, I carried this idea one step further by arguing that standard length words would be a higher correlate of the number of thoughts than actual words.

Fran: You are saying that a passage that contains 200 words probably has more thoughts in it than a passage that contains 150 words. However, if we want a better indicator of the number of thoughts, we should count the number of standard length words in the passage.

Carver: That's correct.

Fran: I'm not sure that I agree with this, but at least I understand it now.

Carver: Once these assumptions are made, it necessarily follows that the number of standard length sentences in a passage (S_p) would be a better indicant of T_p than s_p;

$$T_p = f(s_p) \tag{30}$$

is not as good as

$$T_p = f(S_p). \tag{31}$$

Therefore, a good indicator of rate in thoughts per minute should be one that is measured in standard length sentences per minute,

$$\tilde{R} \cong \frac{S_p}{t}. \tag{32}$$

The end result that we want is a good estimate of A and a good estimate of R. I presented the case earlier, in Topic 1, for using s_c/s_p to estimate A. It should provide a good measure of A because

$$\frac{T_c}{T_p} \cong \frac{s_c}{s_p} \qquad \text{from Equation (26).}$$

I have now, in Topic 2, presented the case for using S_p/t as an indicator of rate since

$$\frac{T_p}{t} \cong \frac{S_p}{t}. \tag{33}$$

Fran: I have tried to follow your arguments, and I have not been able to detect any flaws, but it is still unsettling to me that you use a standard length sentence. However, rather than try to present any counterarguments now, I will simply say that I am withholding judgment on this matter until I have had a chance to study the situation more thoroughly.

Let me see if I can summarize what you have been telling me. What you want is a measure of rate in thoughts presented each minute and a measure of accuracy in thoughts comprehended per thoughts presented. However, thoughts are not directly observable — cannot be empirically measured in a direct way. So, you have developed empirical techniques for estimating each of these variables. Accuracy may be measured in a variety of ways, but one of the most important ways is to estimate the proportion of sentences comprehended. Your method for estimating rate in thoughts per minute is to use standard length sentences. The best way of measuring rate in standard length sentences per minute would probably involve counting syllables and converting them into standard length sentences using a standard number of syllables per standard length sentence. Syllables would be best because you contend that rate is paced by an internal articulation rate, which would be constant in syllables per minute. However, because it is easier to count letterspaces, and because letterspaces are so highly correlated with syllables, you have recommended that rate be measured in standard length words per minute and then converted into standard length sentences.

Carver: That's right. As you will see in Study I, there are data that indicate that there are 1.67 syllables per standard length word, on the average. With this transformation constant, it would be easy to convert back and forth between syllables per minute and standard length words per minute.

Topic 3 – Estimating R_r

Now, I am ready to talk about the measurement of R_r, rauding rate.

One way to measure R_r would be simply to ask people to "read" passages at their normal, natural, typical, or comfortable rate, and if Law I of rauding theory is valid most people should execute their rauding process. When each person finishes the passage, we can simply count the number of standard length sentences and divide that by the time taken to finish the passage,

$$\tilde{R}_r \cong \frac{S_p}{t}. \qquad (34)$$

In this situation, the rate of passage presentation, R, is considered to be equal to the rauding rate, R_r. I used this technique in Study I except rate was expressed in Wpm instead of Spm,

$$\text{Wpm} = \text{Spm} \times \frac{100}{6}. \qquad (35)$$

Another more indirect technique would be to give a person a rate of reading test, the score on which had been correlated with an estimate of $\tilde{R}_r$ so that the test scores could be converted into $\tilde{R}_r$. For example, suppose you get a score of 191 on a rate of reading test; from a table in the manual for the test it may be possible to convert this 191 score into an estimated rauding rate of 317 Wpm or $R_r = 19.0$ Spm. This technique was used in Study III. Any questions?

Fran: No. You estimate rate one way by simply observing how fast people read passages under ordinary or normal circumstances. You estimate rate another way by seeing how fast they can perform on a reading rate test that has been correlated with actual reading rates so a score on the test can be used to provide a predicted rauding rate.

Carver: Correct.

Topic 4 – Estimating $\tilde{A}_r$

Carver: Let's move on to the fourth topic, ways of getting $\tilde{A}_r$. I mentioned at the outset that A_r was a function of the rauding difficulty of the passage and rauding ability of the reader. I have chosen to measure these variables using a grade equivalent scale. This means that I measure the ability of the rauder in grade equivalents. For example, Joe's rauding ability is Grade 9 and Jill's rauding ability is Grade 11. Passage difficulty is measured the same way. One passage may be at Grade 5 difficulty and another passage may be at Grade 13 difficulty. When rauding ability is measured in grade equivalents and when rauding difficulty is measured in grade equivalents, then it is possible to go to a table that is included in the original presentation of rauding theory and obtain a value for $\tilde{A}_r$. The numbers in the table were obtained empirically in a manner that could definitely be improved. However, until I or someone else provides a better way of getting a measure of $\tilde{A}_r$, this will have to do.

Fran: Would you explain how you got the numbers in the table?

Carver: I'd rather not take the time to do that now, since it has already been explained in the original presentation of the theory. I hope to have a better technique operating very soon so this one will no longer be operational.

Topics 5 and 6 – Estimating G_a and G_d

Fran: Will you answer questions about measuring rauding ability and rauding difficulty, the next two topics?

Carver: Yes. I will do that.

By the way, I used the symbol G_a to designate rauding ability measured in grade equivalents and the symbol G_d to designate rauding difficulty, also measured in grade equivalents. For Joe, $G_a = 9$, and for Jill, $G_a = 11$. For the first passage I mentioned earlier, $G_d = 5$, and for the second, $G_d = 13$. If Jill was given the first passage, you could go to a table and find that $\tilde{A}_r = .87$ when $\tilde{G}_a = 11$ and $\tilde{G}_d = 5$. You may notice whenever you look at that table that there are also values for $\tilde{L}_a$ and $\tilde{L}_d$. These are simply symbols I used to designate 6 school levels of ability and difficulty. I lumped grades 1-3 together to get Level 1, grades 4-6 became Level 2, grades 7-9 became Level 3, grades 10-12 became Level 4, grades 13-15 became Level 5, and 16-18 became Level 6. So, if $G_a = 4$, then $L_a = 2$, and if $G_d = 15$, then $L_d = 5$. This lumping of ability and difficulty is convenient for certain data analyses and interpretations. For example, it is convenient to study what people at $L_a = 3$ do when they are presented with passages at $L_d = 3$ and interpret the results as reflecting upon what happens when individuals at the junior high level of rauding ability are presented passages at the junior high level of rauding difficulty.

Fran: Does it make any difference to you how $\tilde{G}_a$ and $\tilde{G}_d$ are measured when your table is used to get $\tilde{A}_r$?

Carver: The answer to that question is yes and no. The table was produced using certain standardized techniques for measuring $\tilde{G}_a$ and $\tilde{G}_d$. The National Reading Standards test was used to get $\tilde{G}_a$; I have said elsewhere the manual for the test allows a score on the test to be rescaled to provide a measure of $\tilde{G}_a$. The Rauding Scale for Prose Difficulty was used to determine $\tilde{G}_d$ and the techniques for doing this are also described elsewhere. You may use other standardized tests to get $\tilde{G}_a$ and other readability scales to determine $\tilde{G}_d$ and still get a usable $\tilde{A}_r$ value from the table. The techniques that I used *should* give you more accurate $\tilde{A}_r$ values because the table was developed using these techniques. However, I would not hesitate very long to use the table to test the theory if the only measure of $\tilde{G}_a$ I had available was a grade equivalent score from the Gates-MacGinitie Reading Test and the only measure of $\tilde{G}_d$ I had available came from a grade equivalent score on a Fry Readability Graph.

Fran: It seems to me that the concepts of rauding ability and rauding difficulty have less background rationale than other aspects of rauding theory.

Carver: This is true. My strategy here was to come up with some way of making sense out of comparing reading ability levels and passage difficulty levels so that rauding accuracy could be predicted, relatively accurately. The focus here is much more on making the theory functional — empirically testable and useful. I will not make excuses for its highly empirical nature because I think it makes more sense than any existing procedure for interrelating readability, reading ability, and the accuracy of passage comprehension. Nevertheless, I would be much more satisfied if this part of the theory could be beefed up from a rationalistic standpoint as long as it could be done with no loss in predictive accuracy.

Topic 7 – Rauding Rescaling

Carver: Now I'd like to get to the final topic, the rauding rescaling procedure.

Study IV, of which I will now give you a copy, contains a complete description of this rescaling technique, called the Rauding Rescaling Procedure.[1]

---

1. Ronald P. Carver, "Measuring Absolute Amounts of Reading Comprehension Using the Rauding Rescaling Procedure."

It will be difficult to control my excitement as I describe this procedure to you. It seems to hold great promise. The steps in the procedure have been programmed for computer analysis so that it is now possible to rescale rather automatically. For example, suppose you developed a new type of test for measuring passage comprehension. Then, you obtained five passages that were previously determined to be equal in difficulty. Suppose you gave these five passages to twenty people at five different rates and then you averaged the percentage they got correct at each rate. Suppose the results were as follows:

Rate (Wpm)	Test Score (percent)
1,000.0	20
500.0	40
250.0	60
125.0	70
62.5	75

These rate data must first be converted into minutes per sentence, $1/R$, and accuracy must be a proportion.

Time $1/\bar{R}$	Accuracy $\bar{A}$
.0167	.20
.0333	.40
.0667	.60
.1333	.66
.2667	.70

Then these data may be given to the computer, and the program will rescale these data so that they represent the best available estimates of A. In this example, these data have been rescaled and the resulting rescaled values are as follows:

Rate (Wpm)	Accuracy (Rescaled) $\bar{A}$
1,000.0	.15
500.0	.46
250.0	.77
125.0	.87
62.5	.93

Furthermore, as part of the rescaling process, the rauding rate and the rauding accuracy for these data are also determined, for example,

$$\tilde{R}_r = 261 \text{ Wpm},$$

and

$$\tilde{A}_r = .76.$$

The average error associated with the rescaling process is also provided, for example, 4 percentage points.

Fran: Are you going to tell me how this works?

Carver: I am going to depend upon you to raud Study IV if you want to know the details of how it works. However, you would have to like numbers and equations fairly well to want to follow each step of the procedure. I'll see if I can give you an overview of the procedure that relies very little on mathematical formulas.

Fran: I'd like that.

Carver: First, we need to review. In rauding theory, there is one relationship hypothesized between accuracy, A, and time, $1/R$, when presentation time is less than rauding time; another relationship is hypothesized when presentation time is greater than rauding time — Hypothesis 3 and Hypothesis 4, respectively. These two relationships were expressed in Equations 16 and 19, but I will write them down again for you as a review.

$$A = (A_r R_r) \frac{1}{R} \quad \text{when } t \le t_r \text{ from Equation (16).}$$

$$A = \frac{1/R}{1/R + i} \quad \text{when } t \ge t_r \text{ from Equation (19).}$$

When $t = t_r$, then presentation time equals rauding time, so $R = R_r$ and $A = A_r$. This is the point where the two curves (from Equations 16 and 19) cross or touch when they are plotted on a graph. At this point where $R = R_r$, A equals A_r no matter which of the two equations are used to solve for A. In the rescaling procedure, one of the first things to do is fit the above curves to the data and solve for R_r because that is the point where the two curves cross. The curves are fit using a least squares linear fit for the first equation; remember that a least squares linear fit simply refers to the regression technique associated with the Pearson Product Moment r. The second equation looks more complex, but you will recall that when this relationship is expressed as $1/E$ versus $1/R$ it is also supposed to be linear. So, the fitting procedure also is able to take advantage of using a least square linear fit in this situation, even though it is a little more involved.

Fran: Wait a minute. If you are fitting these curves, you would have to already know R_r to know which data points belong to the first curve and which data points belong to the second curve. It seems to me that you have to know the answer before you can use this solution.

Carver: You are absolutely right! The rauding rescaling procedure handles this problem by applying the rescaling procedure every possible way. For example, Equation 16 would be fit to all the points up to and including a particular data point, and Equation 19 would be fit to all the points subsequent to and including this same data point. Thus, every data point has associated with it this fitting of curves on each side of it. Whenever curves are fit there is always an average of the errors; there are always differences between the actual data points and the theoretically fitted curves, and the average of the errors may be calculated. Rauding theory takes the best fit of all the possible curves that are fit to the data, when "best fit" means the pair of curves using Equations 16 and 19 that produce the smallest average error.

Fran: Okay. That seems to be a reasonable way to provide an objective solution to the curve fitting problem and finding R_r, but you haven't said anything about rescaling yet.

Carver: By assuming that A and $\bar{A}$ are correlated linearly so that

$$A = b\bar{A} + a, \tag{36}$$

the rescaling problem is mainly solved. That is, by making this assumption it is possible to solve for b and a and thereupon transform values of $\bar{A}$ into values of $\tilde{A}$ using

$$\tilde{A} = b\bar{A} + a. \tag{37}$$

The end result of all this is that the $\bar{A}$ values have been transformed into $\bar{A}$ values, and rauding theory can then be properly tested. Note again that this procedure provides an objective technique for estimating R_r and A_r. It also provides supplementary information such as a measure of the sensitivity of the test used and a measure of how well the theory fits the data — the average of the errors made by the theoretical fit.

Fran: I think I have a general idea of what it is possible to do with the rescaling procedure, but I don't see why you are so excited about it.

Carver: Let me see if I can help you understand this by first describing some of the results I obtained when I first used this procedure. Remember the data I described in Study III where four different techniques were used to measure comprehension and all gave approximately the same result?

Fran: Yes. Wasn't that the study where the theoretically predicted values of A were within about 3 percentage points of the empirical measures, on the average?

Carver: Right. The rescaling of the three objective measures that was done in that study was based upon correlations with the understanding judgments. This means that the equations used to rescale the $\bar{A}$ values could be no better than the validity of the understanding judgments as $\bar{A}$ values. Furthermore, this rescaling technique would only work in those situations where you always asked people to make understanding judgments along with giving them an objective test.

The Rauding Rescaling Procedure was applied to these same Study III data, and the three objective tests were rescaled independently of the understanding judgments. The end result was that the rescaled objective tests provided almost exactly the same absolute measure of accuracy as the understanding judgments. Stated in a different but similar way, when the Rauding Rescaling procedure was used on the objective tests, approximately the same estimates of A were obtained as had been obtained before when the correlations with the understanding judgments had been used to rescale the objective tests.

Fran: I still don't get what is so great about that.

Carver: If you have ever had anything to do with measuring reading comprehension you can appreciate that answering 75 percent of the questions correctly on one reading comprehension test probably does *not* mean that your comprehension on that passage was equal to that in another situation where you also answered 75 percent of the questions correctly. This is because it is impossible to compare percent comprehension scores on one test with those on another because some tests are easy and some are difficult. Some people write easy questions on difficult passages and hard questions on easy passages, so you might actually comprehend 90 percent of the thoughts in Passage A and score 50 percent on its test, and you might comprehend 30 percent of the thoughts in Passage B and score 80 percent on its test. In the past there was no way to measure comprehension on an absolute scale. Now we can rescale your 50 percent score on Passage A, $\bar{A}$ = .50, and find that $\bar{A}$ = .90; you actually comprehended about 90 percent of Passage A although your test score was 50 percent. We can also rescale your 80 percent score on Passage B, $\bar{A}$ = .80 and find that $\bar{A}$ = .30; you actually comprehended about 30 percent of Passage B although your test score was 80 percent. This absolute rescaling of empirical indicants of comprehension allows us to determine more precisely how much comprehension of the passage there really was no matter what the test score indicated. It is difficult for me to talk about this topic without using the word "breakthrough" because this is exactly the way I perceive it in terms of establishing rauding research as an "exact science." This rescaling will allow us to clear away much of the fuzziness and bias that prevent us from making precise comparisons. It allows us. . . .

Fran: I have to interrupt you. You are making this procedure sound as though it were in the center ring in the Greatest Show on Earth. Where is all of that objective, unemotional approach to science?

Carver: Don't worry, all of my appropriately critical colleagues will bring me down to earth soon enough.

Fran: Maybe they should. Are you sure that these fantastic results will generalize beyond these Study IV data?

Carver: Well, I have used the procedure on other unpublished data and it seemed to work well there also.

Fran: You have already taught me to avoid being overwhelmed by your authority, Professor. I need to see the data.

Carver: Okay. Perhaps you are right. This idea may eventually end up as a lot of seemingly bright ideas I've had — in the wastebasket! Let me just say that this technique appears to me to hold a lot of promise. If it gets shot down by empirical data, so be it. I just hope that other researchers perceive it to be promising enough to give it a try.

Fran: That seems more realistic.

Carver: I'm not ashamed of my enthusiasm, but I do appreciate your pointing out that the procedure will have to withstand the rigors of research imposed by others besides myself.

As we wind down my attempt to cover rauding theory, let me summarize its current status. It is rationally sound in that its principles seem to make sense. Yet, its strongest aspect is probably the Three Laws of Rauding. The principles behind these three laws may in fact be found to be in error as research rolls on into the immediate future. However, I do not foresee any data being collected in the near future that will force the repeal of these three laws. The data that I have collected taken in conjunction with data that have already been collected by others convince me that these laws are the pillars of rauding theory. The quantified hypotheses seem to hold a great deal of promise, and in my fondest dreams I see these hypotheses receiving such consistent support that they eventually are also regarded as laws.

Fran: Please don't get carried away by your dreams, here toward the end.

Carver: Okay, smarty, go do your homework. Raud Studies I, II, III, and IV and let me know when you are through. Then, we will continue by discussing criticisms of the theory and the implications it has for psycholinguistics, reading instruction, and reading research.

PART II
RAUDING THEORY CRITICISMS
AND IMPLICATIONS

Chapter 9

WHAT ABOUT THOSE CRITICISMS OF RAUDING THEORY?

Fran: It took quite a bit of time, but I am now familiar with all of those empirical studies that support rauding theory. The only thing I did not bother to do was make sure that you did not make any mathematical mistakes in the rescaling procedure used in Study IV. Solving simultaneous equations or quadratic equations is not my cup of tea. Seriously though, I was not able to catch any major flaws in your data collection or data interpretation.

I guess you can say that I now view rauding theory with much less skepticism than I did before. I'm looking forward to seeing how you handle the criticisms others have made as well as some of my own. I not only rauded your original presentation of rauding theory, but I also went back and rauded all of the criticisms of it made by Hill,[1] Pearson and Kamil,[2] as well as your rebuttal[3] and the subsequent rebuttal of Pearson and Kamil.[4] I'm prepared to confront you with every criticism that stands out in my mind to get your reaction.

Carver: That sounds like a good strategy. What is your first critical question?

Fran: Let me comment first. I believe that you have successfully dispelled the major criticisms of Hill by the rationalistic pre-

---

1. Walter Hill, "Concerning Reading Theory: A Reaction to Carver's 'Toward a Theory of Reading Comprehension and Rauding,'" *Reading Research Quarterly, 13:*64-91, 1977-78.

2. P. David Pearson, Michael L. Kamil, "What Hath Carver Raud? A Reaction to Carver's 'Toward a Theory of Reading Comprehension and Rauding,'" *Reading Research Quarterly, 13:*92-115, 1977-78.

3. Ronald P. Carver, "Another Look at Rauding Theory: Response to Hill and Pearson and Kamil," *Reading Research Quarterly, 13:*116-132, 1977-78.

4. P. David Pearson, Michael L. Kamil, "Comments on the Carver-Pearson/Kamil Exchange in Volume 13, Number 1," *Reading Research Quarterly, 13:*254-256, 1977-78.

sentation you have given me. I do not believe there are any major problems with terms being defined in ambiguous ways.

Carver: It is probably impossible to completely eliminate ambiguity, and I am sure I'll have to work more on clearing up ambiguities in the future. But, I'm pleased that you think I was able to handle the definitions of reading, rauding, and the rauding process to your satisfaction.

Fran: Yes, the key to that was the way you discriminate between a process, the rauding process, and the product of the process, rauding. Hill also was critical of the manner by which you presented the theory. He did not think that it communicated well, and he thought it was too long and complicated. I believe that your rationalistic presentation of the theory with its principles, laws, and hypotheses has eliminated these criticisms.

Later, I want to come back to some of Hill's specific criticisms. Now, I'd like to comment upon the major criticisms of Pearson and Kamil.

The criticism that they made that doesn't quite seem right to me, but I'm not sure I can articulate why, involves their advancement of the interactive top-down model of the reading process as somehow deprecating rauding theory. Could you elaborate on this criticism?

Carver: Rauding theory presents a relatively vague model of what goes on during each one-fifth of a second that elapses during a reading fixation. There are no boxes with arrows drawn between them depicting the process. Because of this, rauding theory has been severely criticized — they say it does not *explain* the mechanisms underlying the act of comprehending. By the way, Walter Hill was also critical of this aspect of rauding theory. He said there was nothing in the theory related to the linguistic-cognitive-affective behaviors that enable a person to comprehend. Thus, these critics have contended that rauding theory does not deal with reading comprehension at all. The people who say this have developed an extremely narrow view of what reading comprehension means.

I have talked about comprehension more from a traditional standpoint in reading and reading comprehension measurement. From this standpoint, it seems natural to say that rauding theory is a theory that deals with reading comprehension; it tries to explain why a person comprehends a certain amount of a passage. This is a perfectly legitimate way to talk about reading comprehension, yet some people, influential people, may not accept this. When someone speaks of reading comprehension, these people do not expect to be told about explanations and predictions dealing with the amount of a passage that has been comprehended. Instead, they are looking for a more advanced model that explains the comprehension act or process. They are interested in the intricacies of "why" someone comprehends, whereas in rauding theory the act of comprehension is assumed. In rauding theory, it is given that people can and do understand most sentences they encounter whether they are written or spoken. Rather than trying to explain why a person can comprehend a sentence, rauding theory tries to explain as much as is necessary about the comprehension process to explain why varying amounts of passages are comprehended by individuals of varying ability when the passages vary in difficulty and are read for varying amounts of time.

Because rauding theory does not try to explain why certain things occur during reading, for example, why a word will be pronounced and comprehended one way in one context and another way in another context, it has been chided as not explaining anything at all. The most important empirical fact that rauding theory explains is why people who are told to read passages for a fixed amount of time at their normal rate tend to cover equal amounts of material in passages of varying difficulties. Conventional wisdom in reading does not explain this; instead, from conventional wisdom one would have predicted a quite different result. Current theory about eye movements during reading does not explain this and in most cases would predict quite a different result. Rauding theory was developed to explain those empirical facts, and it seems to be especially good in this regard, as it should be.

Rauding theory attempts to explain and predict quantifiable aspects of reading comprehension, and traditionalists in reading have not been interested in doing this. My goal is to expand reading research beyond its sole concern with qualitative hypotheses. I want reading researchers to consider quantitative hypotheses. I want to try to explain quantitative things about reading. Before Lavoisier, chemistry was a qualitative science somewhat analogous to current reading research. The transformation of chemistry was monumental after Lavoisier forced a focus upon quantitative hypotheses in chemistry. Of course, I'm daydreaming again, but I think it is time for reading researchers to see what gains can be made by entertaining quantitative hypotheses.

Fran: But I'm overwhelmed by numbers when I encounter a reading research report now!

Carver: Don't be misled into thinking that because an analysis of variance was used that all the numbers that result indicate that the research was focused upon the quantitative aspects of reading. Not at all. I do not think that you can show me a single reading research article where the focus of the research was upon a certain absolute amount of some entity. Rather, hypotheses about qualitative differences are tested by finding out if two things that are supposedly qualitatively different tend to produce a different amount of something. If it does, then the inferences from the numbers generated have much to do with qualities and little to do with quantities. Stated differently, how many hypotheses about reading have you seen tested lately that were in the form of mathematical equations?

Fran: None! With the exception of yours!

Carver: The reading researchers who are up on the latest in cognitive models of reading do not know how to respond to rauding theory. Since it did not spring from one of their paradigms, but it does use some of the same terminology such as "comprehension," there is a knee-jerk reaction to say that it doesn't explain anything. My own opinion is that there is plenty of room for current cognitive research on reading models as well as rauding theory. They should be complementary. I certainly do not see them as natural competitors except in those instances where conflicting predictions are made. Much of what is currently being explored in terms of reading models will fit comfortably within the rauding process part of rauding theory. Most reading models would profit greatly by discriminating among the processes involved in scanning, skimming, rauding, studying, and memorizing.

Yes, it disturbs me greatly to hear that rauding theory does not explain anything because from my point of view it systematically explains a great deal about reading, certainly more than any competitive set of organized ideas of which I am aware. It explains why different amounts of passages are comprehended by different readers. It explains why a person comprehends different amounts of a passage when allowed different amounts of time to read. It explains . . .

Fran: Whoa! I think you have more than made your point that it was a red herring to suggest that rauding theory did not explain anything. However, wasn't it a legitimate criticism that rauding theory does not explain much about the reading process?

Carver: To the extent that the rauding process is the most frequently occurring type of reading process, it was not a legitimate criticism. If you remember, I went to a great deal of trouble to explain how the rauding process worked — the steps involved in the operation of the rauding process, how people talked to themselves during the rauding process at a constant rate, and how eye movements were shaped during long periods of rauding. I would very much disagree that rauding theory did not have a great deal of importance to say about the single most important reading process of all existing reading processes. However, I would like to point out that the rauding process is only a part of rauding theory. Rauding theory was not designed *primarily* to explain the rauding process, so it should not be expected to provide the definitive word in this regard. In my opinion, those who criticize rauding theory from the standpoint of being a model of "the" reading comprehension process have a very narrow and parochial view of what is important or relevant in reading research and theory.

Fran: That covers my general comments and questions regarding the published criticisms of rauding theory. Now, I'm ready to ask you about some of the particulars. Hill says he cannot be sure that you intended to generalize rauding theory to "life" reading circumstances. Did you intend to do this?

Carver: I'm disappointed that my writings left some doubt in Hill's mind and in your mind. Let there be no misunderstanding about this. I do intend for rauding theory to apply to real life reading situations. In fact, that is the major emphasis of rauding theory — that most reading is rauding. Therefore, rauding theory should have many practical applications, since it purports to apply to 80 to 90 percent of all the reading that occurs in this world.

Fran: I thought that was the case, but I wanted to get the point cleared up before I went on to subsequent Hill criticisms. He suggests that if you are interested in real world reading, then many people in reading will "raise an eyebrow" when they encounter some parts of rauding theory.

Carver: Refresh my memory, will you please?

Fran: First, he suggests that it is questionable whether typical adult readers comprehend most of the complete thoughts in passages as they read them.

Carver: My translation of this criticism is that he is suggesting that rauding does not occur most of the time that reading occurs. This is a criticism that could be dealt with empirically. My position is that the probability is so high that rauding is predominant that it is not an efficient use of my time to conduct such an empirical investigation. Yet, for those who have the inclination, I would applaud their efforts to collect relevant data.

Fran: Hill also questions the idea that the efficiency of comprehension is related to the number of thoughts comprehended during a certain amount of time and is not related to the usefulness or quality of the thoughts comprehended.

Carver: I realize that this idea is extremely difficult for many people to swallow, especially those who focus upon main ideas or the hierarchical structure of prose. However, I contend that the author of a passage constructs the sentences so as to be able to communicate his/her thoughts in the best manner possible. Of course, the reader may decide at some point that certain of these thoughts are more salient than others — some are worth remembering longer than others because they are more useful — and then switch into a memorizing process that involves rehearsal of certain parts. When we start discussing the relative quality of the thoughts, we are getting away from rauding and into studying and memorizing; we are getting away from the comprehension that is associated with the communication of thoughts and into the recall of previously learned ideas. When rauding, the person is understanding each consecutively presented thought because the person is trying to complete the communication process that was initiated by the author. Thus, during this process, it seems to be reasonable to assume that each thought may be counted as equal when investigating the efficiency of the rauding process.

By analogy, the existing qualitative differences between thoughts are disregarded when considering efficiency just as existing qualitative differences between cars on an assembly line would be disregarded when calculating the efficiency of production. The number of cars coming down the assembly line (thoughts presented, by analogy) each day divided by twenty-four would give you the rate of production in cars per hour. However, if some of the cars were rejects — not marketable in the form they came off the assembly line — then you would want to divide the number of marketable cars (thoughts comprehended, by analogy) by twenty-four hours to give the efficiency of production in cars per hour. Again, this procedure makes a great deal of sense if you are interested in certain quantitative things about car production even though each car may be qualitatively different because it is a different style, size, or model. I think that most thoughts have enough in common with most other thoughts to place them in the same category and count them when trying to investigate meaningfully the efficiency with which thoughts are comprehended. You may disagree. If so, it probably suggests that you place little value upon the quantitative aspects of reading efficiency, because by ignoring certain of the qualitative differences between thoughts, rauding theory is able to explain and predict a great deal about certain quantitative things.

It makes a great deal of sense to me to refuse to consider all the thoughts in a passage to be equal if you are doing research on studying, which requires that an individual be able to recall certain thoughts contained in passages that an instructor considers important. Thus, for investigators who are interested in the recall of main ideas or for investigators interested in what and how one remembers what was read in a passage, then it would be impossible to buy the assumption that each thought was equal. To illustrate this point consider a study of free recall by Pichert and Anderson (1977). Subjects studied a 350-word passage for two minutes. They concluded that " . . . it is inappropriate to speak as though the importance of an idea unit were an invariant structural property of the text" (p. 314).[5] Yet, if prose learning researchers look down their noses at an assumption of thoughts as equal units in rauding theory, it suggests to me that they need to broaden their horizons.

Let's jump over to the field of physics so I can better make my point about needing to broaden horizons. When dealing with the reflection of light, then light may be considered to consist essentially of "light rays," and this assumption will work well in explaining lenses and shadows. If you consider light to consist of waves, you will find that this helps you explain the colors of the rainbow and the fuzziness of shadows. Yet, if you want to explain how photo cells work — those contraptions that are used in some stores to set off a bell when a customer walks into the store — then you had better consider light to consist of small particles or corpuscles. Yet, light is a ray *or* a wave *or* a particle; it cannot be all three at once. The moral of this story is that there seems to be no inherent problem with rauding theory considering thoughts to be qualitatively equal when investigating the efficiency of comprehension. Reading researchers who are not investigating rauding may find it impossible to consider sentences to be qualitatively equal, but this should have no unfavorable consequence for rauding theory.

Fran: I think I've got the idea! Stated in the current vernacular, different strokes for different folks!

Carver: Yes. In this case, I would say different assumptions about thoughts when dealing with different reading processes such as scanning, skimming, rauding, studying, memorizing. It is my understanding that in some areas of the physical sciences,

---

5. James W. Pichert, Richard C. Anderson, "Taking Different Perspectives on a Story," *Journal of Educational Psychology*, 69:309-315, 1977.

atoms were at one time considered to be perfectly elastic while in other areas they were not. This is only a superficial inconsistency that comes from a failure to understand that different assumptions are being used to solve different types of scientific problems. My fondest hope is that my critics will not get hung up on this facet of rauding theory and thereupon overlook the power of the theory. The power of the theory comes from being able to observe certain things about individuals and certain things about passages, for example, G_a, G_d, and R_r, and then predict certain other observables when the passage and the individual interact — such as the accuracy, rate, and efficiency with which the individuals will comprehend passages when they are allowed certain amounts of time to attempt to raud.

Fran: Hill also questioned the ideas that (a) reading rate is constant, (b) that comprehension improves with additional time to read, and (c) that mature readers cannot comprehend passages by reading any more efficiently than by listening to them. However, Hill did not have access to Studies I, II, and III when he made these criticisms. I think you have successfully refuted each of these criticisms the best way possible — with the data presented in Studies I, II, III, and IV.

Carver: Agreed! The idea that reading rate is constant is directly supported in Study I and indirectly supported in Studies II, III, and IV. The idea that comprehension improves with additional time spent reading a passage is directly supported in Study II and indirectly supported in Study III and Study IV. The idea that readers cannot comprehend thoughts in passages any more efficiently by reading than by auding is directly supported in Study II.

Fran: I am now ready to dig into some of the details of the Pearson and Kamil criticisms. First I'm going to ask you about some of the criticisms they made in their initial response to your original article but to which you did not respond in your rebuttal. Then, I will ask you about some of the criticisms they made in their rebuttal article to which you did not formally respond either.

They point out that you specifically exclude skimming and studying, for example, from your theory. They go on to say, and I quote: "As educators we ought to be wary of a model that excludes what we hope students occasionally do."

Carver: P and K, that is Pearson and Kamil, seem to be saying that all educators should be on guard against a theorist trying to describe and explain certain features about reading but not including pedagogical points that are important to educators. P and K are suggesting that because educators hope students in school will learn to skim and to study, any attempt to explain how the accuracy of comprehension of passages varies from person to person and from passage to passage during the operation of the rauding process should be suspect. I find this criticism of P and K to be especially inappropriate.

Fran: Pearson and Kamil contend that when the rauding ability of the reader, G_a, exceeds the rauding difficulty of the passage, G_d, by a large amount so that reading is very easy, rauding theory will "fall apart." They go on to argue that less time should be required to read easier material.

Carver: Do you remember Study II where college students who could raud at the college level, $G_d = 13$, 14, and 15, were given passages to read and aud at Grade 5 and Grade 8?

Fran: Yes, that was the optimal rate of reading study.

Carver: Did rauding theory fall apart?

Fran: No, I thought those data were especially supportive of the theory.

Carver: Instead of falling apart, rauding theory was supported at *each* level of material difficulty. This criticism reminds one of the followers of Aristotle and how they could not accept Galileo's idea that a 10 lb. ball and a 1 lb. ball would reach the ground at the same time when dropped simultaneously from the same point. It was so logical that the heavier ball would drop faster that they paid little attention to the collection of empirical data that might be counter to their beautiful logic. It is so logical that easy material should be read faster than harder material (after all, don't we know that highly frequent words are recognized faster than less frequent words); yet, the data collected does seem not to be in accordance with this logic at all.

Fran: Maybe Pearson and Kamil will in fact change their minds when they have a chance to raud Study I; or, have you considered the possibility that these data are specific to Carver and cannot be replicated by other researchers?

Carver: Ouch . . . That hurt! But, you are right! We do need to wait and see what happens when other people test the hypotheses of rauding theory. Don't forget, however, that there are other researchers who have already collected data that indicate that people tend to read at a constant rate.

Fran: Moving on, P and K say, and I quote: "Until and unless rauding theory becomes more sophisticated, it will never achieve the goal to which all reading theories should aspire — explanation of the most remarkable and complex set of human behaviors."

Carver: There are several points relevant here, some of which I have talked about before.

I think P and K are criticizing rauding theory because it is not a theory of reading that includes scanning, skimming, studying, and memorizing. Should you expect a scientist who is trying to develop a quantitative theory about oxygen (rauding by analogy), which is a part of air (reading by analogy), to provide an encompassing theory about air at the same time? On the other hand, since reading is made up mostly of rauding, a theory about rauding should go a long way toward the explanation, prediction, and control of how much comprehension takes place when individuals read.

I also think P and K simply cannot entertain the idea that rauding theory assumes that comprehension happens instead of explaining how it happens. They were sorely disappointed because they expected this newly advanced theory dealing with "reading comprehension" to focus more upon the intricate, internal cognitive processes that qualitatively explain why comprehension takes place.

Fran: P and K say that the data that you presented in your original presentation of rauding theory " . . . shows clear evidence that reading is *more* efficient at rates over 300 words per minute" and that you should have revised your emphasis on rate and the hypotheses concerning rate.

Carver: Obviously, I did not make it clear enough that there was an important difference between actual rate and average rate. P and K did not understand the difference between manipulating time and rate. When presentation time is manipulated, as it was with the reading data, the subjects proceed at their own rate, the rauding rate, R_r, and the R values are simply the average rate at which the passage was read. In this situation, actual rate is not manipulated; average rate is what is manipulated via manipulation of time. Thus, it is inappropriate to interpret the constantly high E values, which correspond to high R values, as reflecting a high E_r value. P and K were simply confused by the complexities of rauding theory — they did not understand that Hypothesis 3 and Hypothesis 4 are both appropriate when time is manipulated but Hypothesis 3 is not appropriate when rate is manipulated. They did not understand that rauding theory makes its most complete explanations of why people comprehend varying amounts of passages when they are not forced to read at any particular rate — rate is not manipulated but instead the individuals are allowed to read at a rate of their own choosing for a fixed amount of time. If presentation time is manipulated to produce different R values, then the actual rate at which the individual operated the rauding process is still most likely to be R_r instead of R. However, if the words in the passage are presented at different rates by using motion picture film, for example, then the actual rate, R, that the passage will be covered by the individual is *not* likely to be R_r. Whether it is best to manipulate average rate or actual rate depends solely upon your purpose, and for many research purposes it is not appropriate to manipulate rate. If these complexities were unnecessary, then they should have been revised out of the theory so that P and K as well as others would not be unnecessarily confused. Unfortunately, the complexity is inherent in the nature of the phenomena and cannot be taken care of completely by clearer explanations. I will confess that my original explanations of these theoretical ideas were not nearly clear enough. With the aid of hindsight, I think P and K's confusions were as much my fault as theirs.

Fran: At the end of their criticisms, P and K seem to be saying that rauding theory chooses to use mathematical formulas to express theoretical relationships in a precise and refutable manner but that it is too early to search for mathematical precision, and that to consider rauding theory seriously has a dangerously high probability of retarding progress. P and K do tone this down at the very end by wondering out loud whether they are being too hypercritical. Yet they raised a scary specter in the eyes of the cursory reader. I'd like to hear your response to this.

Carver: A premier philosopher of science, Nagel,[6] has pointed out that a theoretical formulation, such as rauding theory, is not free from dangers because it may be a potential intellectual trap as well as an invaluable intellectual tool. For example, the notion of "force" in physics has always produced intellectual traps because of its association with the sensation of strain in muscular effort (a person holding a 100 lb. weight exerts zero force, as force is defined in physics). Nagel goes on to say that there is no way of telling in advance whether we have a blind alley or a heuristically valuable new idea; we must try out the theoretical ideas and see how they work. P and K seem to be saying that rauding theory may lead us down a blind alley, so maybe we should not try it. I think this idea is incompatible with scientific progress.

Fran: You have covered everything I wanted to hear about from the P and K initial paper. Now, I'd like to move on to your response to some of the things that were in their rebuttal paper. P and K have argued that the theory cannot possibly reach its goal of accurately predicting comprehension because the distinction you make between reading and rauding will *logically* prevent this from happening.

Carver: Their position is that to use rauding theory it is necessary to have an a priori means of determining whether an individual is engaging in reading in general or rauding in particular. They simply are not willing to make a conceptual distinction between rauding and all the other possible types of reading — scanning, skimming, studying, memorizing. If most reading researchers are of this same opinion (that it is detrimental to research in reading to make a major distinction between a skimming process and the rauding process, for example), then Pearson and Kamil have indeed made a devastating criticism of

---

6. Ernest Nagel, *The Structure of Science: Problems in the Logic of Scientific Explanation* (New York, Harcourt, Brace & World, Inc., 1961).

rauding theory. If reading researchers do *not* agree with Pearson and Kamil on this point, they can reflect this disagreement in several ways. Researchers investigating rauding can attempt to give instructions that stimulate their subjects to read in the same manner they would ordinarily read were they not in an experiment. Researchers can refrain from generalizing about rauding if the experimental tasks were not conducive to rauding — in situations, for example, that clearly require memorizing sentences or scanning letters in words. Researchers can show more awareness of the time limits used in their studies; short time limits in some tasks may yield skimming strategies, and long time limits may yield studying strategies. Researchers can design the demand characteristics of their experiments so as to allow more clearly, on an a priori basis, the classification of the experimental activities into rauding or some other type of reading.

On this point about making a priori distinctions between reading and rauding, Pearson and Kamil seem to confuse a rather straightforward aspect of rauding theory or, for that matter, any theory. Before a theory can be expected to be appropriate, certain a priori conditions have to be given. Before the theoretical relationship between distance and time for free-falling bodies can be used to make accurate predictions ($d = \frac{1}{2}gt^2$), one has to have a body released from a point away from the earth; the body may not be a feather, for example, unless the feather is released in a vacuum. Predictions made from rauding theory about the comprehension of thoughts in a passage are not relevant when one has a reading situation in which something other than rauding would be expected to occur. Rauding theory would not be expected to be relevant in situations such as (a) studying a textbook so as to pass test in a course, (b) scanning a phone book for a name, (c) memorizing the Gettysburg Address, or (d) skimming to obtain some information about an entire article because there was not enough time to raud the article.

Fran: Pearson and Kamil also offered their opinion that they would prefer a unified theory of reading that incorporated and theoretically distinguished reading and rauding, rather than two separate theories.

Carver: I would agree with them on this point. It would be nice to have a quantified theory that applied to all reading instead of just its most important and prevalent subtype. I would also *prefer* to have a unified theory that incorporated all reading and all listening together with associated pedagogical techniques, and then I would toss in concept learning, motor learning, affective learning, etc., etc. Should we criticize Galileo because he did not expand his theoretical ideas about the force of gravity to include the moon, planets, and stars, as Newton did many years later? Should we deprecate Newton because he did not foresee that his ideas about absolute motion were only appropriate for relatively slow speeds, as Einstein noted centuries later in his Theory of Relativity?

Anyone can dream and criticize someone else for not accomplishing one's own dreams. Remember, a theory should be held accountable for explaining those facts that it purports to explain and how well it is able to predict new experimental facts. P and K are going well beyond those criteria when they indicate that the theory does not deal with all facets of reading.

Fran: P and K questioned the value of using time to "estimate rate," when alternate experimental methods of manipulating rate are available.

Carver: On this point, the critics have demonstrated again that they did not grasp the full scope and thrust of rauding theory.

Fran: Let's go on to P and K's criticisms involving statistical significance. They seem to argue that statistical significance testing is needed to decide how well a curve fits the data.

Carver: Yes, they do! Yet, they also seem to acknowledge that the most important principle involved is the amount of error involved in the fit. However, they do not trust my judgment or even their own in this matter. When I reported that, on the average, the amount of error was only 2 percentage points on a scale that has a total of 100 percentage points, this was meaningless to them unless they could test it for statistical significance. This is not just the stance of these two critics but also represents most of the research community. Too many researchers are paralyzed without a test of statistical significance, placing blind faith in an objective mathematical procedure that does not do what you think it does. Rather than elaborate, I will simply refer you to my own lengthy criticisms of statistical significance[7] where I argue that research would be better off without it and that manuscripts which contain such tests should be rejected just as we now reject the idea of publishing manuscripts that contain raw data because it is trivial information.

Fran: What do Pearson and Kamil mean when they say that "curve fitting is an empirical procedure"?

Carver: I think they are arguing that the proper strategy is to try to fit as many curves as possible, such as exponential functions, and then choose the curve that fits best. This idea is completely counter to the reason for developing theory in the first place. The power of good theory is in being able to explain and describe a phenomenon well enough to accurately predict what will happen in the future. If we are always using a trial and error process where we try out new curves and choose the one that fits the present data best, we are likely to make little progress, because we will always be postdicting instead of predicting. On this point, Pearson and Kamil show signs of being pure empiricists in the Skinnerian sense, which seems counter to their previous admonitions that we should make a better effort to theorize well. Their arguments relevant to statistical significance and curve fitting do not hold water for me.

Fran: I've saved P and K's criticisms about *standard length sentences* until last. I'd like to hear you respond to these criticisms.

Carver: Yes, I'm glad you brought up this point because it deserves a great deal of elaboration. One way to look at the measurement of thoughts by counting character spaces is to consider it "arbitrary." Torgerson[8] calls this type of arbitrary measurement, measurement by fiat. We use measurement by fiat whenever we have a common sense concept that seems to be important but we do not know how to measure it directly. I want to measure the number of thoughts in a passage, and that seems very important to me, yet I do not know how to do it directly.

---

7. Ronald P. Carver, "The Case Against Statistical Significance Testing," *Harvard Educational Review*, 48:378-399, 1978.

8. Warren S. Torgerson, *Theory and Methods of Scaling* (New York, John Wiley & Sons, 1958).

Therefore, I take the bull by the horns, so to speak, and use measurement by fiat. I have said that we can estimate the number of thoughts in a passage by counting the number of standard length sentences. Torgerson has the following to say about this measurement by fiat procedure: "One thing should be emphasized, however, there is certainly nothing *wrong* or *logically incorrect* with the procedure. It has lead to a great many results of both practical and theoretical significance" (pp. 23, 24).

Pearson and Kamil have pointed out the obvious — that one standard length sentence might contain two actual sentences. I can't help but think of an analogy in this situation. Whoever it was that suggested that we use the standard length "foot" as a measure of distance might have been plagued by the same kind of deprecating comments. Can't you imagine someone laughing and saying the following.

> You're trying to tell me that this is a foot when it is obvious that this distance will cover two of my son's feet. You are trying to tell me that this is a foot when I know perfectly well what the properties of a foot are — this thing you call a foot has no toes and definitely will not fill a sock. What is this nonsense about a standard length foot?

I think the above ridiculous analogy has relevance in the present situation. I am being criticized for using the standard length sentence as an indicator of the number of thoughts contained in a passage, and I don't think this is any more illogical than using a standard length foot to indicate distance. If I am overlooking something fundamental about measurement in this situation, I hope you or someone else sets me straight.

Let me give you another analogy! The strength of gravitational attraction between two particular objects of a given mass depends on the distance between their centers. This means that if I want to know how much the earth's gravity is pulling on me, I need to know how far it is from the center of the earth to me. Now, does this mean that gravity is a force that is concentrated in a small point at the very center of the earth? No, that is ridiculous. It is a simple fact that we can make some rather accurate estimates about the pull of the earth's gravity if we consider it to be concentrated at the center. I am saying that I can make some rather accurate predictions about the degree to which passages are comprehended when they are read if I consider thoughts to come in standard lengths. This does not mean that thoughts necessarily do come in standard lengths (just as the force of gravity is not necessarily concentrated at the center of the earth).

Fran: My guess is that Pearson and Kamil will be able to come up with a rebuttal to some of these counterarguments of yours.

Carver: Yes, it is always worth remembering that there are two sides to almost every story, and we will have to wait to hear what I have overlooked from the point of view of Pearson and Kamil as well as Hill.

Fran: The final set of criticisms are those which I heard discussed in the hall during a research convention I attended. I made notes, and I will continue to ask you about them one by one. First, let me hear again your reactions to the criticisms that rauding theory does not take into account a host of important variables, such as motivation and the linguistic complexity of sentences.

Carver: Again, I am trying to come up with laws that include what I think are the most important variables for explaining and predicting the amount of passage comprehension during a certain length of time allowed for rauding. I think that motivation and the linguistic complexity of sentences are good examples of specific factors influencing rauding that can be safely ignored when trying to account for important general factors.

The laws of rauding theory are idealistic in the same sense as laws in physical sciences are idealistic. The law that states that the period of a pendulum is proportional to the square root of its length neglects the weight of the rod supporting the pendulum and neglects the friction between the rod and its support. In many real world situations these neglected factors may not be negligible so that predictions about the period of the pendulum are somewhat in error. However, it is shortsighted to suggest that the law is no good or not helpful just because these factors, which sometimes are important, were not provided for in the law. My contention is that most of the time when people raud we can predict fairly accurately how much of a passage they will comprehend without resorting to an account of factors such as motivation and linguistic complexity that sometimes do affect comprehension.

Fran: I overheard one researcher saying that your ideas were interesting but since they were based on a "limited print driven view of reading" this precluded their being very important.

Carver: Here we are again, fussing over models of "the" reading process! In a sense, the rauding process is print driven. Rauding theory holds that during the rauding process each consecutive word is perceived and articulated — no word is skipped either visually or subvocally. Thus, the printed words pace the process via their perception and internal articulation. The person who made this critical remark about rauding theory has convinced himself or herself that any reading process that can be labeled as print driven is outmoded and therefore cannot possibly be valid or important. I think this type of casual brush-off is unbecoming to a serious researcher.

Fran: For one set of extensive critical remarks, I jotted them all down. I would like to give them to you now in their entirety.

> The reader and text variables which have been studied and reported so extensively in recent years are not accounted for. He must account for linguistic complexity and existing schema as well as for perceptual processing. The model of reading is not interactive, nor does it account for prior knowledge, text structure and cohesion. Since sentences seem to be the important unit of thought, it is surprising that sentence complexity isn't accounted for. Since this theory is in conflict with the hypothesis testing view, for good readers, more widely accepted today (Hochberg, Mackworth, Kintsch, Bransford and Franks), this discrepancy should be accounted for in some way.

Carver: Wow! I'm glad I don't know who it was that said all of that. If I am arguing with "anonymous" then I worry less about being extremely tactful in my response!

First, let's deal with the purported failure to account for reader variables such as existing schema and prior knowledge. I disagree that the theory completely disregards these variables. These variables are lumped together into the G_a variable, rauding ability, that I described earlier. It is true that this is a very global way of dealing with these variables. As I mentioned before, a person who has a G_a of 7 and is presented a passage at G_d

= 7 for rauding will have a single A_r value. Thus, the theory does not take into account that some individuals with a G_a of 7 who are reading some passages with a G_d of 7 will have a higher A_r than other individuals at G_a = 7 who are reading other passages at G_d = 7; this is because some of these individuals will have more background knowledge, or relevant schema, than others for certain of these passages.

It may occur to you that the theory could be refined by having G_a measured in certain topic areas such as social studies, physical sciences, etc. I doubt if this refinement would satisfy this critic, but it does show you the direction rauding theory might take if I wanted to be more responsive to this type of criticism. I think rauding theory presently does an admirable job of explaining and predicting how much of a particular passage individuals will comprehend when they are given a particular amount of time. I think rauding theory accomplishes a great deal in terms of predictive power without adding further refinements involving background knowledge and schema variables that admittedly do have some effect upon the degree of passage comprehension.

I have already talked about how rauding theory relates to passage variables such as linguistic complexity, text structure, cohension, and sentence complexity. Remember, I said that these variables were lumped together into the G_d variable — passage difficulty. So, I have accounted for these variables in rauding theory. Admittedly, I have not accounted for them in a way that will suit this critic, because this critic is undoubtedly not quantitatively oriented but instead is a champion of current schema research and current text structure research. If I wanted to refine rauding theory, then this G_d variable would have to be reanalyzed until it reflected various important dimensions of passages, such as sentence complexity and text structure. Then, I would somehow have to be able to combine all of this passage difficulty information just discussed to give me a single pre-dicted A_r value. If I were able to do this I *might* make this critic happy, but my guess is that this critic is so involved in his or her own areas of interest that this achievement would still not be considered important, mainly because the critic will not accept the idea that it is important to be able to predict *amounts* of passage comprehension.

Finally, this critic appears to be sold on the latest interactive models of the reading process that are consistent with the hypothesis testing view. Since rauding theory does not embrace the latest interactive models and since it is counter to the hypothesis testing view, then this critic believes that rauding theory should be given little attention or assigned little importance. Let me remind you that Study I, which you read earlier, deals specifically with the hypothesis testing view of reading, which has been around a long time, so rauding theory does try to account for discrepancies between it and this view.

Fran: Right, but don't forget this critic did not have a chance to see Study I before these comments were made.

Carver: Okay, but don't you forget that these kinds of criticisms suggest one of two things; either the critic does not understand rauding theory well enough to provide valid criticisms or the critic is so narrow in his/her views of what is important in reading research that he/she cannot consider rauding theory as opening up new vistas of information and knowledge. To try to explain and predict quantitative aspects of rauding should not be looked upon with distaste because it does not incorporate or explain all aspects of reading.

Fran: You seem to be preaching, Professor Carver.

Carver: Sorry about that, let's move on.

Note: After this manuscript explaining rauding theory had been written, the following review and analysis of the original 1977-78 presentation of rauding theory was published: Hans U. Grundin, "Further Steps Toward a Theory of Comprehension and Rauding," *Instructional Science*, 9:15-41, 1980.

Chapter 10

WHAT ABOUT PSYCHOLINGUISTICS AND READING?

Fran: I have read some of Frank Smith's ideas about reading and psycholinguistics,[1, 2] and it seems to me that rauding theory is in conflict with a number of his ideas.

Carver: You're right. There are a number of ways that rauding theory and his ideas, derived from psycholinguistics, are in opposition. Smith seems to contend that reading does not involve any internal articulation of the words. He argues that a "fluent" reader does not identify each word but gets the meaning from the words without identifying each and every word. He says that readers "predict" their way through a passage of text, using the redundancy of the passage to lessen the amount of visual information required to read. He says that identifying each word — pronouncing each word — is "hard work" and is only used when the reader encounters reading material that "goes beyond his previous experience." He says that " . . . reading cannot be considered a process of decoding written symbols into speech; it is neither necessary nor possible for writing to be comprehended this way."

As I interpret Smith's ideas, he is saying that there is no qualitative difference between rauding and skimming, and reading and auding have little or nothing in common. In short, these ideas of Smith's are incompatible with the concept of rauding. He certainly would not agree that typical reading is facilitated by subvocalization, or that typical reading is paced by an internal articulation rate, or that there is an optimal rate of reading that is the same as the optimal rate of auding.

---

1. Frank Smith, *Understanding Reading: A Psycholinguistic Analysis of Reading and Learning to Read* (New York, Holt, Rinehart and Winston, 1971).
2. Frank Smith, *Psycholinguistics and Reading* (New York, Holt, Rinehart and Winston, 1973).

146

Rauding theory presents an alternative to Frank Smith's view of reading. Frank Smith's view of reading could easily be considered "the" contemporary view of reading. Because his views are different from that of rauding theory, I think we should analyze his views in some detail so you can see very precisely how rauding theory is different and why.

In one of Smith's books he reprinted George Miller's article from the 1965 *American Psychologist;* this article has acted as a foundation for psycholinguistic research and theory. One of the things that Miller said was that researchers should talk more about "hypothesis testing instead of discrimination learning." It was natural, I suppose, for the hypothesis testing view of reading to evolve from this comment of Miller's. This perspective is one that has blurred any differences between the rauding process and a skimming process, for example. I suppose it is part of the reason why there have not been any lines drawn between scanning, skimming, rauding, studying, and memorizing. Instead of the qualitative differences put forward in rauding theory, all reading seems to have been viewed as of the same fundamental form, involving hypothesis testing. The hypothesis testing view is also a major part of what I have called the contemporary view of reading.

So that you will know more precisely what it is that rauding theory is in opposition to, I would like for you to take a look at these statements regarding the hypothesis testing view, which were presented in a government publication and made by a distinguished researcher, Ralph Haber.[3]

> Typical readers do not look at every word, nor in fact do they need to see every word in order to read continuously. This should be expected since reading is a very good example of constructive perception. The reader needs to develop some sense about what the sentence or paragraph, or page is about. This implies that the fixations should be much closer together (almost on every word) near the beginning of a paragraph or when it is clear from the context that the content is about to change. As the reader develops a sense of what it is he is reading, he can use this to

3. Ralph Haber, Visual Perception, in L. L. Elliott, ed., Psychology and the Handicapped Child (Washington, U.S. Office of Education, DHEW Pub. No. (OE) 73-05000, 1974).

guide his constructions. It is as if we form a hypothesis about what we will find on the page and then check it every few words to verify it, revising the hypothesis as we go along. If the content is quite predictable based on the hypothesis, less verification is needed and eye movements can be farther apart leading to an increase in reading speed!" (p. 67)

You can see that this hypothesis testing view is diametrically opposed to rauding theory. It presents a picture of individuals continually changing rates based upon what happens following continually formulated hypotheses.

Let's get back to Smith's ideas, because they further describe the distinctive features of this hypothesis testing view of reading that has evolved from psycholinquistics. The one point that Smith hits harder than any other in his writings is that it is a fallacy to consider reading to be *decoding from written symbol to sound.* Rauding theory is easily in agreement with Smith on this point. This proposition is much too simple, and some of the arguments Smith puts forward against it seem easy to swallow. This simple conception of reading seems to suggest that all one has to do to read is to be able to pronounce the words. It turns out, however, that this is simply a "strawperson" that fronts for Smith's more drastic views about decoding to sound. He *appears* to cleverly demonstrate that certain words cannot be pronounced correctly unless we have some knowledge about their meaning. He uses the following two sentences to illustrate his point:

1. He sang in a beautiful bass although he could not read music.
2. He read the notice that fishing for bass was permitted.

He says that we could not pronounce "bass" and "read" correctly in these two sentences unless we selected the proper pronunciation on the basis of meaning. He says that we go from what the words say to what they mean without saying them. He concludes that (1) saying the words is an unnecessary appendage, and (2) saying the words is not part of silent reading. At least saying the words, according to Smith, is not a part of the ordinary or typical silent reading that is done by fluent readers, because if we cannot read with the immediate comprehension that occurs without saying the words, then we "soon feel tired or bored."

It is one thing for Smith to argue that we must have some information about the meaning of a word before we know how to pronounce it, and it is another thing to draw the two conclusions that (1) pronouncing the word is unnecessary and that (2) it is not done. The only evidence I can remember that Smith advanced for his assertion that the words are not subvocalized — not internally articulated or not individually identified — is that some readers are able to read at rates much greater than words can possibly be internally articulated or individually identified. Smith is not the only one to fall into this particular trap. Many others have done the same thing. They drag out the purported "fact" that people can read at 500, 1,000, or 10,000 words per minute. This is *not* a fact. It is *nonsense*. There exists no empirical data of which I am aware, and I make it my business to look for such data, that justifies saying that people can read at 500, 1,000, or 10,000 words per minute unless "read" means skimming or scanning. People can skim at any such rate — people can skim at these rates but they cannot raud at these rates. It cannot be denied that people get meaning from print while skimming. Ulric Neisser, in his classic and influential book *Cognitive Psychology,*[4] defined reading as "externally guided thinking," and this has provided justification for skimming to be called reading. This global and vague definition also allows scanning, studying, and memorizing to be called reading. Carried even further, this definition would allow the thinking that was stimulated by watching a baseball game to be called reading. Such an imprecise definition allows all of the important differences among scanning, skimming, rauding, studying, and memorizing to be glossed over. Finally, it allows the erroneous conclusion to be drawn that the typical silent reading done by skilled readers does not involve any internal articulation or identification of each word.

I cannot agree at all with the idea that skilled readers typically infer or correctly predict the meaning of all the words without identifying all of them individually. I have yet to see published the type of study that would support these ideas of Smith's, which were stimulated by psycholinguistics. Such a study might

---

4. Ulric Neisser, *Cognitive Psychology* (New York, Appleton-Century-Crofts, 1967).

involve a group of typical college students who are given passages to raud at their rauding rate of 300 words per minute. The passages would have been chosen so that the students do very well on the subsequent comprehension questions, but comparable students who have not rauded the passages score about chance on the questions. Then, these same passages and questions would be given to some of these "fluent" readers of Smith's who have never encountered these passages or questions before. These fluent readers would be given enough time to read the passage so that their average rate of reading is 1,000 words per minute. As I understand Smith's ideas, he would predict that his "fluent" readers would do just as well on the comprehension measures as the typical college student who plods along at 300 words per minute, probably identifying every word along the way.

I think it is worthwhile to review the empirical evidence that Smith does advance to support his arguments. He refers to a piece of research done by E. Llewellyn Thomas, a physician, that was published in a little book on speed reading.[5] If you are lucky enough to obtain the original version of this article you will find it interesting. Dr. Thomas photographed the eye movements of a speed reader and showed how he skipped all over a page while proceeding at an average rate of 10,000 words per minute. It should be of little surprise to anyone that a person who was executing a skimming process could cover 10,000 words per minute while skipping erratically over the words. What would be phenomenal is evidence that the person actually comprehended as much during this frenetic feat as did typical college students who rauded it at their typical rate of 300 words per minute.

Fran: Didn't Thomas measure this speed reader's comprehension?

Carver: I was astonished to find out when I rauded this research report that no attempt was made to check on comprehension. Instead, this researcher reported that "No tests of

5. E. Llewellyn Thomas, "Eye Movements in Speed Reading," in R. G. Stauffer, ed., *Speed Reading: Practices and Procedures* (Proceedings of the 44th Annual Education Conference sponsored by the School of Education, University of Delaware, Newark, 1963).

comprehension were made in this trial but *S* was tested on a later occasion by Dr. Russell Stauffer, and showed good comprehension."

Fran: You mean that there was nothing done in the way of determining what informational benefits accrued to this highly skilled reader while covering the passage at 10,000 words per minute?

Carver: Right, and I don't want you to forget that this is the only empirical evidence I have ever seen referenced in connection with bolstering the case that skilled readers can "read" with good comprehension at high rates. Although there seem to be no empirical data to back up the idea that some people can comprehend most of the sentences in an unfamiliar passage at rates above 1,000 words per minute, some researchers still "believe" that this is an established fact. I have seen numerous instances in which this bogus fact was used to argue against the internal articulation and identification of each word during "reading." For example, Bower[6] states, "Consider the fact that a skilled reader can read with comprehension at rates of more than 1,000 words per minute" (p. 135). He goes on to use this so-called "fact" to rule out any kind of auditory transformation during reading, such as subvocalization or internal articulation. It is interesting that Bower reported on some "reading" research of his own that involved " . . . eight fast readers (speeds of 1,000 words per minute or more) . . . " (p. 139), but he never took the trouble to explain how it was operationally determined that these people "read" at 1,000 words per minute. Most likely these people were skimming with the level of sentence comprehension that would be expected from skimming. Again, let me repeat: it is not a fact that people can raud at 1,000 words per minute even though it is easy to concede that many people can skim or scan at 1,000 words per minute.

Ulric Neisser is another person who uses the skimming argument against the internal articulation of each word. He says, " . . . to identify a word or a letter is to pronounce its name in

---

6. Thomas G. R. Bower, "Reading by Eye," in H. Levin and J. P. Williams, eds., *Basic Studies on Reading* (New York, Basic Books, 1970).

inner or outer speech. . . . Since many people read appreciably faster than 300 or even 600 words per minute, they surely do not identify every word. . . . "

Again, don't fail to note that the argument goes like this:

1. People can read at rates greater than 600 words per minute.
2. It is impossible for people to say words to themselves at rates greater than 600 words per minute.
3. Therefore, it is wrong to consider reading to involve saying words to oneself.

Notice what happens to this argument when reading is not considered to be a fundamental entity but is made up of components with different attributes. I can concede that it is a fact that people can "skim" at rates greater than 600 words per minute. However, if the skimming process is in fact qualitatively different from the rauding process, then one cannot reasonably generalize about rauding given a fact about skimming, just as it is unreasonable to generalize about nitrogen given a fact about oxygen.

Although you may be more familiar with Smith's hypothesis testing ideas, which are presented in the framework of psycholinguistics, it was actually Neisser who, in 1967, laid the groundwork for these ideas, which blur any distinctions between skimming and rauding. In his book, Neisser presents some of the most meticulous interpretations of empirical data I have ever seen. However, those interpretations of data were primarily relevant to visual perception, in general. He devotes about two pages of his 351-page book to "reading," and the single bit of empirical research that he mentions in connection with reading involves scanning word lists. Those of us who consider the scanning of word lists and the skimming of passages to involve processes that are qualitatively different from the rauding process would be forced to say that this little section of Neisser's on "reading" is full of nonsense.

Neisser concludes this section on reading with the following statement: "For the present, rapid reading represents an achievement as impossible in theory as it is commonplace in practice." That was 1967! In 1980 I can make the following statement: For the present, rapid reading is skimming and it represents an achievement that is as possible in rauding theory as it is uncommon in practice.

Fran: You seem to be using pure argument to combat pure argument. Can't you refer to any data since 1967 that would support your side or Neisser's side?

Carver: Don't forget Study I and Study II, which indicated no support for the hypothesis testing view! Rather than review the literature, I will refer to the most recent and most relevant research of which I am aware. In a 1979 technical report, McConkie, Hogaboam, Wolverton, and Zola have summarized a great deal of recent eye movement research. They state, "There is no evidence here that the reader is essentially anticipating what is to come next and then acquiring only that visual information necessary to confirm or reject the prediction" (p. 15).[7] Anticipation is what is involved in the hypothesis testing view, and I think this eye movement research summarized by McConkie et al. provides more than pure argument against the hypothesis testing view.

Another recent publication is relevant to this issue. Wildman and Kling reviewed the literature relevant to anticipation in reading.[8] By almost all standards, this was an excellent critical review of the literature relevant to the issues surrounding anticipation effects in reading. From the standpoint of rauding theory, however, there are serious limitations to what we can gain from the analyses of Wildman and Kling. The entire review seems to be based upon certain unstated premises, such as (a) there are no qualitative differences among scanning, skimming, rauding, studying, and memorizing that are important enough to make distinctions between them, and (b) rauding rate is not constant. If this review, or a future one, could be focused upon

7. George W. McConkie, Thomas W. Hogaboam, Gary S. Wolverton, David Zola, "Toward the Use of Eye Movements in the Study of Language Processing," Technical Report No. 134 (Urbana, Illinois, Center for the Study of Reading, University of Illinois, 1979).

8. Daniel M. Wildman, Martin Kling, "Semantic, Syntactic, and Special Anticipation in Reading," *Reading Research Quarterly, 14:*128-164, 1978-79.

research and theory relevant only to rauding situations, I feel confident that there would be much less of a problem in seeing through the fog created by the results of many studies in various reading situations. For example, Wildman and Kling refer to an " . . . important and data-rich eye movement study by Wanat (1976) . . . " (p. 144). From Wanat's[9] study Wildman and Kling concluded that "Clearly the anticipated surface structure determined the observed saccadic and regressive eye movements" (p. 144). If this generalization applied to rauding situations, then it would not be supportive of rauding theory. So, I closely checked Wanat's methodology. He studied eye movements while people read isolated sentences. The subjects were instructed to read the sentences "naturally and attend to their meaning," and then they were told that they might be asked to paraphrase the sentences. The instructions were seemingly amenable to rauding. However, the isolated sentences presented for reading were not conducive to rauding. For example, one sentence was, "On the picnic the girls that Bill teased saw the child." This sentence is a little puzzle that requires studying. It seems reasonable to question whether any results from this research would generalize to a rauding situation. Indeed, these data certainly should not be interpreted as indicating that anticipated surface structure influences saccidic and regressive eye movements during rauding, because the subjects were probably using a studying process on these sentences.

Wildman and Kling did scrutinize in detail the hypothesis testing view, which they called the "Hypothesis Test Position," and they too found it lacking. However, all of their conclusions need to be reevaluated because they are based upon a potpourri of anticipation type research relevent to reading; a re-review of the research relevant to rauding would undoubtedly produce different conclusions. For example, there seems to be little reason to expect that the role of anticipation will be the same when skimming a passage, rauding a passage, or studying a

---

9. Stanley F. Wanat, "Relations Between Language and Visual Processing," in H. Singer and R. B. Ruddell, eds., *Theoretical Models and Processes of Reading* (Newark, Delaware, International Reading Association, 1976), pp. 108-136.

passage. In summary, I have seen no empirical evidence that would support the hypothesis testing view for *all* of the various types of reading, and I have seen plenty of evidence against it, such as that reviewed by McConkie et al. mentioned earlier.

I also interpret existing empirical data as indicating that individuals typically do say each of the words in a passage to themselves as they raud, and I challenge you or anyone else to present data or arguments against this. In my original theory article I reviewed research that supports the case for the internal articulation of words during reading. I have concluded that Smith and others are wrong when they argue or hint or suggest that typical reading does not involve saying each word to oneself. It seems perfectly possible to me for Smith and cohorts to be correct when they say that the meaning of a word can be recognized without any prior internal articulation of the words. Just as we can recognize a familiar face and all the meaning that goes with it *without* remembering the name that goes with the face, so it seems possible to recognize the meaning of the printed word "dog" without saying "dog" to oneself or prior to saying "dog" to oneself. However, just because I have conceded that saying the word "dog" in certain isolated situations may be an unnecessary appendage for reacting to its meaning, I have not conceded that saying the word *is* an unnecessary appendage in rauding situations. On the contrary, I have argued that saying the words to oneself is a facilitator of the rauding process. Exactly why this should be so is almost beyond my range of speculation; it is presently at the frontier of knowledge production. The reason for the facilitative effect probably has something to do with the phonological encoding that facilitates certain memory functions which occur during rauding. Cunningham and Cunningham[10] recently conducted some research in this area, and they suggested that " . . . fluent readers proceed from 'print to meaning to sound to memory.'" The point I am trying to make here is that there is no solid evidence or rationale to support Smith's view that saying the words to oneself is an unnecessary appendage for

---

10. Patricia M. Cunningham, James W. Cunningham, "Investigating the 'Print to Meaning Hypothesis'" *Twenty-seventh Yearbook of the National Reading Conference* (Clemson, South Carolina, National Reading Conference, 1978).

rauding. Maybe, just maybe, saying the words does not facilitate scanning or skimming, but that is an issue that goes beyond where I want to go.

Now, let's get back to the very first idea of Smith's where he argued that it was necessary to ascertain the meaning of a word prior to knowing how to pronounce it. You have already gotten the point, I hope, that this argument really has little or no consequence for rauding theory, since rauding theory only holds that comprehending thoughts in a passage is facilitated and paced by the saying of the words to oneself. It is not crucial to rauding theory whether saying the word comes before, during, or after the meaning of the words is ascertained. Although this argument is not crucial to rauding theory at the present, I would like to respond to this argument, since it does have relevance to the intricacies of the rauding process.

It seems to me that it is not necessary to concede to Smith that the meaning of a word must be determined prior to deciding how it should be pronounced. Consider the word "bass" in Smith's example that I showed you earlier. The pronunciation of this word is determined by the prior context as well as the meaning. We learn to pronounce a word differently in different contexts even when the meaning is the same. For example, if I am reading out loud to children in Boston I may pronounce certain words different from the way I would pronounce them to children in Kansas City — for "Cuba" I may say "Q-ber" in Boston and "Q-ba" in Kansas City. The meaning is the same, but the situational context changes the pronunciation. Similarly, from the context of a passage, I have learned that "bass" is pronounced "b-ass" in "fishy" contexts and "b-ace" in "musical" contexts. Thus, I will not concede that Smith has demonstrated his point that meaning must *precede* pronunciation. We could just as reasonably predict that "bass" would be pronounced "b-ass" in fishy situations even if meaning followed pronunciation.

Fran: Okay, I think you have convinced me that nothing that Frank Smith has presented about decoding to sound should be considered as providing evidence against rauding theory. When I conceded early on that there were important qualitative differences between skimming and rauding, Frank Smith's arguments became ambiguous and unconvincing because he never made these crucial distinctions in his presentations. Do you have anything else to say about Frank Smith's ideas?

Carver: At the moment, all I can think of is that Frank Smith is to be applauded for his creative theorizing about reading based upon what he knew about psycholinguistics. From his perspective, it seemed imminently logical that people would vary their rate so as to take advantage of the degree of redundancy in the material being read. Unfortunately, another theory has been slain by the facts, just as the Aristolian idea that a 10 lb. ball would fall faster than a 1 lb. ball was slain by Galileo when he found that these two balls fall at the same speed.

Fran: Shouldn't credit be given to Smith and others who advanced these theoretical ideas and thereupon stimulated certain empirical facts to be developed via research?

Carver: Yes, Smith deserves a great deal of credit for advancing these theoretical ideas about reading. We should also recognize that Frank Smith's ideas do not encompass the entire topic of psycholinguistics and reading. However, I do think it is safe to say that all of the theorizing and research involving psycholinguistics and reading has been hampered by two primary failures: (1) a failure of omission when qualitative distinctions were not made among different reading processes, such as scanning, skimming, rauding, studying, and memorizing, and (2) a failure of commission when the commonality between reading and auding was purposely disregarded. In short, I think that in the future, reading research that involves psycholinguistics will profit greatly if there is a discrimination made between reading and rauding.

Chapter 11

WHAT DOES RAUDING THEORY IMPLY FOR READING INSTRUCTION?

Carver: Rauding theory is not a theory of instruction in reading or rauding. However, it does have certain implications for instruction. The close connection between auding and reading that is amplified by the concept rauding bears close scrutiny. Both reading and auding involve talking to oneself. Since talking and auding naturally precede reading for most children, it follows that reading ability will lag behind auding ability during the early years in school. In fact, initial reading instruction need only be concerned with helping the child learn to recognize visually the words that the child can already recognize auditorily. Thus, for students in the early grades, A_r for materials at Grades 1, 2, and 3 difficulty will probably be higher — greater than .75 — if the materials are presented auditorily; however, if the materials are presented visually, A_r will probably be close to .00. Stated differently, children in the early grades can auditorily raud a large number of passages but can visually raud, via print, only a very small number of passages.

It would seem that early reading instruction would probably profit from the sole use of materials that the child could raud if presented auditorily. This means that it does not seem wise to overload the child with the problem of trying to understand unfamiliar or difficult thoughts when the problem of recognizing the words requires so much effort and attention. In the beginning, then, it would seem best to give children sentences that they can already raud auditorily when trying to help them learn to recognize words visually. To make the point more concrete, country children should not be given instructional materials that only a city child can auditorily raud, and city children should not be given instructional materials that only a country child can raud. This rule should hold up until the child has learned to raud visually almost everything that the child

158

already knows how to raud auditorily, probably somewhere around $G_a = 4\text{-}6$. From this point on, A_r for auding a passage will approximately equal A_r for reading a passage. From this point on, it would seem to be misleading to contend that children need to be taught rauding skills or that further improvement in rauding involves skill building. Instead, improvement in rauding ability probably depends more upon increases in knowledge. The skill of visual rauding has already advanced to the point where it is comparable with auditory rauding.

If you want to improve rauding ability, the primary way is to increase the person's background knowledge. This can be accomplished in several ways. For example, if you want to increase a child's A_r for a passage dealing with interworkings of a daily newspaper, then you could talk to the child about this topic ahead of time, explaining what certain words mean and what you already know about newspapers. This prior knowledge, or schema, about newspapers, will help the child raud the passage even though there was no prior reading practice that dealt specifically with the topic of newspapers. An alternative way of increasing the child's A_r for this particular passage would be to take the child on a guided tour of the offices and printing plant of a local newspaper. This experience will also provide background knowledge that will increase A_r for this passage that deals with newspapers. Probably the best way of increasing A_r for this particular passage, in terms of low expenditures of time, effort, and resources, would be to give the child another passage dealing with newspapers that covers the same general material in simpler and more explanatory ways. Then, when the passage in question is administered, most of the terms and ideas would already be familiar, and the child would have little difficulty rauding the passage.

Although there are many avenues for increasing a child's background so that he/she will have a higher A_r value for passages that are related to that knowledge, the most efficient way is for the child to acquire this knowledge vicariously through the experiences and written thoughts of others. Thus, it follows that the better rauders get to be better rauders primarily because of the background knowledge they have acquired from their numerous vicarious experiences obtained through rauding.

Fran: These ideas you have been presenting seem very similar to those espoused in a book I looked at some time ago.

Carver: Was it entitled *Auding and Reading* by Tom Sticht and co-workers?[1]

Fran: That was it!

Carver: Yes, most of these ideas of mine about instruction are not new. I'll also recommend another article by John Carroll,[2] which says some of the things I have been saying.

Fran: Earlier, you were talking about the accuracy of the rauding process from the standpoint of G_a, rauding ability. You, in effect, were saying that the best way to increase G_a is to increase a person's background knowledge. However, according to rauding theory, a person's rauding ability is most succinctly formulated in his/her rauding efficiency, E_r, and E_r is made up of two components A_r and R_r. You haven't said anything about R_r.

Carver: Rauding rate is dependent upon how fast a person can say the words to himself/herself and still comprehend the sentences. This ability is probably not readily changed by environmental factors such as instruction. Rauding rate is probably a structural property of the brain and not easily manipulated. No matter how much I practiced and no matter how hard I tried, I was always the slowest runner when I ran footraces with children my age. With excellent instructors and with extensive training, my running speed could no doubt have been improved somewhat — but at great cost in terms of my time and the instructor's time. Similarly, it does not seem reasonable that excellent instruction or Olympian practice will cause much change in the rauding rate of most people.

Fran: Then why do we find research that indicates that the reading rate of children tends to increase with each grade in school. Surely that must have something to do with their practice or instruction.

---

1. Thomas G. Sticht, Lawrence J. Beck, Robert N. Hauke, Glenn M. Kleiman, James H. James, *Auding and Reading* (Alexandria, Virginia, Human Resources Research Organization, 1974).

2. John B. Carroll, "Developmental Parameters of Reading Comprehension," in J. T. Guthrie, ed., *Cognition, Curriculum, and Comprehension* (Newark, Delaware, International Reading Association, 1977), pp. 1-15.

Carver: Possibly, but I doubt it. I think it is more likely that you are confusing correlation with causation. It seems more likely to me that the children are maturing in many ways and that all of their brain processes are becoming faster, not just reading. I think they are able to raud faster because they are physically maturing, and this has little or nothing to do with their practice or instruction in reading. My idea could be tested in a hypothetical experiment by looking at the increase in rauding rate for two groups, one that received reading training and one that simply received comparable auding experiences but did no reading. My hypotheses would be that the group that reads would not experience greater gains in rauding rate than the group that did not read but only auded.

Fran: Are you saying that you think training in reading rate is of little or no benefit?

Carver: For children who are beginning to read — their auditory A_r is higher than the visual A_r — then practice in recognizing the words visually should be of benefit; automaticity training should be of benefit to this group.

Fran: I have heard of the word "automaticity," but I'm not sure I know what you mean.

Carver: I'll not take the time to explain it in any detail; you can look at some of the work by Jay Samuels for that.[3] Very simply, it involves extensive practice in decoding so that certain words are overlearned to the point that they can be recognized very fast.

As I was saying, automaticity training should be effective as long as the G_a for visual rauding is below G_a for auditory rauding. However, once visual parity has been achieved — the visual A_r is approximately equal to the auditory A_r for almost all passages — then I would say that rauding rate training is superfluous. I'd like to add that I have not seen any research data that would convince me otherwise.

Fran: What about the speed reading training that is given commercially and at most colleges and universities?

Carver: These courses vary considerably in content, but for

---

3. David LaBerge, S. Jay Samuels, "Toward a Theory of Automatic Information Processing in Reading," *Cognitive Psychology*, 6:293-323, 1974.

the most part I would say that they are a great waste of time, talent, energy, and money.

Fran: Why?

Carver: Because there is no sound evidence that speed reading training is able to increase a person's rauding rate. Also, there are no *rationally defensible* reasons for expecting speed reading training to be able to increase a person's rauding rate. For almost all people, the ability to understand sentences is not limited by a bottleneck associated with eye movements but instead is limited by an internal brain process that works equally well with auditory material. Therefore, why should practice in reading fast increase rauding rate? There is no reason to expect that practice in reading fast will improve a person's auditory rauding rate, and since auditory rauding rate is the same as visual rauding rate for most people, then it follows that reading fast cannot be expected to increase the rauding rate of most people.

Fran: From some of your other published articles, I'm not too surprised that you don't have many kind words to say about speed reading training!

Carver: I cannot see speed reading training justified at all in terms of improving rauding rate for most people. However, speed reading training is just great for someone who cannot skim efficiently and wants help in accomplishing this feat. In fact, speed reading training should help you learn to skip over words without trying to build complete thoughts out of them, and it should help in training your eyes to skip habitually without requiring part of your attention. So, as skimming training, speed reading instruction is great! I just wish speed reading instructors would realize this and stop making their students feel guilty as they return to their regular rauding rate when they want to understand what the author is trying to communicate.

Every time I talk to someone who has had speed reading training or has known someone who has, I always hear a remark about how hard it is to keep in practice and how easy it is to lapse into old reading habits. With the aid of rauding theory, this phenomenon is relatively easy to explain. The rate they raud is a highly overlearned habit that is extremely efficient for understanding an author's thoughts. Since most of the time most people desire to understand the thoughts that authors have written in the form of sentences, they would be foolish to attempt to skim and accomplish this purpose. Therefore, it is easy to return to the old eye movement habits because they are most efficient most of the time.

Fran: You seem to be pleased that your theory handled that explanation so well.

Carver: I am, but that is not too surprising, since one of the motivations behind the development of rauding theory was to try to take some of the nonsense out of speed reading.

Fran: I've been around some of these speed reading classes. They don't spend all of their time practicing going fast. They don't spend all of their time with skimming practice.

Carver: You're right! Especially those classes associated with universities. They will spend a great deal of their time on study skills. I have no objection to the teaching of study skills to people who need them — notetaking, underlining, previewing, etc. I also understand that many people who are responsible for these courses only call them speed reading courses to hook the student into a class where the instructors can help them learn more about study skills. However, I think this is false advertising; it is not truth in labeling. This tactic may come back to haunt people in reading because there will be a crisis in confidence when the word eventually gets around that speed reading is simply skimming in disguise.

Fran: My, you have the zeal of a missionary when it comes to knocking speed reading.

Carver: Somebody has to say that the emperor has no clothes on. If indeed some people perceive the emperor as actually having clothes on, I will eagerly wait to see their evidence. Meanwhile, all the research data and theoretical rationale indicate to me that speed reading training will not help people raud better!

Let me try to summarize what I have been saying. I estimate that less than 1 person in every 100 will find that they can raud better as a result of speed reading training. However, probably twenty-five out of every 100 people who volunteer to take this training will skim better and study better as a result of the training. Rate training for people under age sixteen is likely to be a waste of time because these students have little need to skim. *The best way to improve the rauding of people under sixteen is to get them to raud more and study more so they will become wiser and therefore better rauders. The more they raud the wiser they become, and the wiser they become the more they are capable of rauding.* For those students who raud poorly compared to their peers but who have a G_a around 4-6, it is not surprising that most efforts to teach them to raud better fail. This is because they are not lacking in skills associated with rauding. It is doubtful if these poor readers could auditorily raud what they have trouble visually rauding. Therefore, what we have is not a "reading" problem, per se, but a knowledge problem, and deficits in knowledge are extremely difficult to overcome for people who raud poorly. People who raud well can very quickly make up knowledge deficits by finding an appropriate book and then rauding it or studying it. They can profit from the experiences of others and thereby increase their experience vicariously. However, people who cannot raud will have to get their experiential knowledge first hand, and this is often very time consuming or impossible. Thus, we have a vicious circle. The good rauders raud more and become better rauders. The poor rauders raud less and fall further behind in their rauding ability. I see no shortcut way to solve this problem. However, I think that if the reality of the problem is recognized, then someone is more likely to find a solution in the distant future.

Fran: This doesn't seem to be a new idea. I'm sure I've read other people who have expressed this same general idea. Instead of a national reading problem I've heard it said that we have a national "thinking" problem.

Carver: No, the idea is far from new. I simply wanted to discuss it in the context of rauding theory.

Fran: It seems to me that you have some very definite opinions about reading instruction some of which seem to be implied from rauding theory and others of which are questionably related to rauding theory.

Carver: For a person who is a self-avowed nonexpert in reading instruction, I have said too much already. I had better move on before I get into deep trouble with my freely given speculations.

Fran: Before you move on, I'd like you to comment some more about flexibility. Many people think that there is no single or typical reading rate, that if a person does read at a single rate something is wrong, and that reading flexibility should be taught to students in school.

Carver: I realize that I am fighting an uphill battle here. For example, over thirty-five years ago the following statement appeared in the *Journal of Educational Psychology:* "It is apparent, then that there is no meaningful 'single' reading rate (in words per minute) for any given individual, but that, instead, he reads at many different rates, each specific to a different purpose" (p. 450).[4] A more recent version of the same general idea was expressed in this same journal by Samuels and Dahl in 1975[5] They said, "The attempt of some researchers to find a typical reading rate would appear to be an ill-conceived notion in light of current conceptualizations regarding passage difficulty and purpose of reading" (pp. 42-43). I can agree with part of the above statement as long as there is no intention for "reading" to mean "rauding." There is no single reading rate because the purpose of each type of reading is different; different purposes should lead to the execution of different processes, which in turn proceed at different rates. I cannot agree, as you already know (a) that there is no "typical" reading rate, (b) that rauding does not proceed at a constant rate for most people, or (c) that variations in passage difficulty always produce different rauding rates.

If flexibility means knowing how and when to scan, skim, raud, study, or memorize, then I am all in favor of flexibility instruction for college and secondary level students who have not already learned when and how to do these things. If flexibility means knowing how and when to change rates when the

---

4. Paul Bloomers, E. F. Lindquist, "Rate of Comprehension of Reading: Its Measurement and Its Relation to Comprehension," *Journal of Educational Psychology, 35*:440-473, 1944.

5. S. Jay Samuels, Patricia R. Dahl, "Purpose for Reading and Flexibility of Reading Rate," *Journal of Educational Psychology, 67*:38-43, 1975.

purpose is to understand thoughts contained in the sentences of a raudable passage, then I am vehemently opposed to flexibility instruction.

A recent article by Phyllis Miller on flexibility instruction provides an example of how current thought about flexibility is counter to rauding theory.[6] Miller starts out by saying that "an individual does not have a single base rate" (p. 73). A single base rate is exactly what a person does have according to rauding theory. She goes on to indicate that she does not take flexibility to mean the shifting of gears from one process to another but instead opts for the fluid drive model; she says that " . . . the flexibility concept is based on the assumption that a reader is capable of using a range of rates, in the sense of a continuum, i.e., from slower to faster" (p. 74). These ideas are completely counter to rauding theory, and the conclusions she draws about flexibility instruction are only valid if her view is correct and the view from rauding theory is wrong.

I would say that those people concerned with reading flexibility instruction are caught right in the middle of the issue regarding which view of reading is correct, the conventional viewpoint or the viewpoint espoused by rauding theory. After the dust has settled on this issue, those people proclaiming what to do about flexibility instruction will have a firmer foundation upon which to build.

Fran: So you don't think anything is wrong with a student who reads at a constant rate, and you don't care much for flexibility instruction.

Carver: That is not exactly a correct summary of my opinion. It is true that I don't think anything is wrong with a person who rauds at a constant rate. However, if a person always executes the rauding process even in those situations where it would be more appropriate to use a studying or skimming process, this would be wrong. As for flexibility instruction, I would say that at present it is almost always based on an incorrect view of reading,

---

6. Phyllis A. Miller, "Considering Flexibility of Reading Rate for Assessment and Development of Efficient Reading Behavior," in S. Jay Samuels, ed., *What Research Has to Say about Reading Instruction* (Newark, Delaware, International Reading Association, 1978), pp. 72-83.

and because of this, it is either a waste of time or even detrimental to students.

Fran: Does rauding theory have implications for those instructors who are trying to get people to learn new things? I'm
thinking of training directors in industry who are responsible
for helping employees learn something new by getting them to
read training manuals or textbooks.

Carver: You are taking me dangerously close to the edge of
rauding and into studying. This situation you've outlined is also
very close to what goes on in a college or university when a
textbook is required reading for a course. What I can do is show
you how to estimate what proportion of a textbook a student
should have comprehended after one attempt to raud it. I can
also estimate how long it would take the student to finish this
attempt to raud the book once. Since the accuracy of comprehension is likely to be low in this type of a situation, let's base our
estimates on *two* attempts to raud the book.

Fran: I do think it would help me if you would go through
some of the details of how you would make these estimates.

Carver: First, you need an estimate of G_a. If the students were
college freshmen, I probably would estimate their average rauding ability to be $G_a = 13$, unless I had some reason to expect my
group to be above or below average. Of course, if I could manage
it I would get a more objective estimate by administering a
standardized reading test that allowed me to convert test scores
into grade equivalents. Once I had obtained my best available
estimate of G_a, I would move on to getting an estimate of the
difficulty of the reading material for the course — an estimate of
G_d. I would probably use a standardized technique, such as a
readability formula, or the Rauding Scale of Prose Difficulty that
I have developed. I would probably sample pages from the book,
get a G_d estimate for each page, and then calculate the mean or
median of these sample pages. With these estimates of G_a and G_d,
I would go next to Table 3 in the original presentation of rauding theory, unless I or someone else had developed a better
technique for estimating A_r and R_r.

Fran: How about using some hypothetical values to illustrate
your points?

Carver: Okay. Suppose my best estimate was 11.4 for G_a and 16.4 for G_d. Entering Table 3 with these values gives me a .13 estimate for A_r and a 14.7 estimate for R_r in Spm, standard length sentences per minute.

The next thing I need to do is estimate the length of the material in standard length sentences. To do this I would probably locate what I considered to be a typical page in terms of length, or words on the page. Then, I would locate three typical length lines on the page and count the total number of letter-spaces, including punctuation marks, on each of these three lines. Then, I would calculate the mean of these three letter-spaces count and multiply this mean by the number of lines on the page to give me an estimate of the number of letterspaces on the page. I would divide this result by 100 to give me the number of standard length sentences on the page. Finally, I would multiply this result by the total number of pages in the material to give me an estimate of the total number of standard length sentences in the material. Let me use some hypothetical values to make the example concrete. Suppose the three lines were 75, 78, and 72 letterspaces long. The mean line length would be 75. With 100 spaces per standard length sentence, this would be 75/100 or .75 standard length sentences per line. Suppose there were 40 lines on the page; 40 × .75 would give 30 standard length sentences per page. Suppose there were 350 pages in the book, so 30 × 350 would give a total of 10,500 standard length sentences in the material. Dividing 10,500 by 14.7 Spm gives 714 minutes or 11.9 hours without breaks. If the student read the material twice, taking a 10 minute break each hour, the actual time spent engaged in the rauding process would be 23.8 hours, but the total time devoted to this learning project would be 28.6 hours. Let's now estimate what A_r would be after the rauding process had operated twice on this material, t = 1428 minutes. The inefficiency constant, i, would be

$$i = \frac{1}{14.7}\left(\frac{1}{.13} - 1\right) = .4552 \quad \text{from equation (20),}$$

and

$$\frac{1}{R} = \frac{1428}{10,500} = .136 \quad \text{from equation (15),}$$

and

$$A = \frac{.136}{.136 + .4552} = .23 \qquad \text{from equation (19).}$$

Thus, we could estimate that the average student in the course might understand 23 percent of the material for the course if the student spent about twenty-nine hours attempting to raud it.

This kind of information might be helpful to curriculum designers and teachers as they make decisions about training materials for a course. My guess is that there would be a number of changes in textbook selections, for example, if practitioners in reading were able to provide these kinds of engineering estimates to those who are responsible for such courses.

Fran: Reading instruction usually focuses upon the teaching of reading — learning to read rather than reading to learn. Are you dealing with a situation that involves reading to learn?

Carver: Yes. I am encroaching upon a studying situation. A studying process should involve more time per standard length sentence. Thus, the estimated 23 percent comprehension represents an estimate based upon the continual operation of the rauding process, and this assumption is of questionable validity. Nevertheless, it is possible to provide some figures that illustrate how much comprehension can be expected under certain time expended situations. It would not be reasonable to expect more than 23 percent comprehension after twenty-nine hours spent on the material. This information is not directly related to reading instruction per se, but it is relevant to those practitioners in reading who might act as consultants in a learning center or a reading center. These are the kind of estimates you might expect from a "reading engineer."

Fran: I think these kinds of objective assessments would strengthen the role of reading practitioners as they give advice to curriculum planners.

Carver: That exhausts my storehouse of information on this topic. I'm ready to talk about the implications of rauding theory for research.

Chapter 12

WHAT DOES RAUDING THEORY IMPLY FOR READING RESEARCH?

Carver: The acceptance of rauding theory implies that reading researchers should be more explicit about when they are investigating rauding and when they are not investigating rauding. Acceptance of the idea that air was not a fundamental property of nature but instead was primarily made up of oxygen and nitrogen forced a change in subsequent research practices. A researcher who was studying the properties of nitrogen would not say that he/she was studying the properties of air. That would not be precise enough. Even though oxygen and nitrogen make up most of air, it would be misleading and wrong to study the lawful events associated with nitrogen and then claim that one was studying air. Also, because it was claimed that air had been studied it would be wrong to imply that the findings applied equally well to each part of air, including oxygen. Likewise, I think it will be a big mistake if reading researchers continue to investigate memorizing processes, studying processes, scanning processes, and skimming processes and say that they are investigating reading, because too often this erroneously implies that what they find is relevant to rauding. In most cases, it will be impossible to make valid inferences about the rauding process by investigating scanning, skimming, studying, and memorizing processes. Furthermore, since rauding is by far the most prevalent type of reading activity engaged in by humans, it also seems that it should receive the largest share of attention. Since studying processes are important for increasing our rauding ability, they also deserve a great deal of attention.

Once a reading researcher has decided which of the reading processes he/she is going to study, then everything about the experimental design should be geared toward making sure that this process was actually what occurred in the experimental situation. For example, suppose a researcher does want to study

170

the rauding process. The instructions given to the student by this rauding researcher should be designed to get the student to execute this process. The consequences of doing the reading should be designed so the person is not forced out of the rauding process by reinforcing a skimming process or a studying process, for example. If very difficult passages are used, it may be much more questionable to infer that the rauding process was executed. This is because individuals are apt to switch into a studying process or even a skimming process if they are not rauding while executing the rauding process. If the amount of time allowed is considerably less than or considerably greater than that required for rauding, it is unlikely that the rauding process will be executed unless specific instructions and conditions are focused on rauding. People may skim if they perceive that they cannot finish the passage using the rauding process, and they may study or even memorize if they have more than enough time to raud. If a passage is only one or two sentences long, or if the passage is very lengthy such as fifty sentences long, it may also be difficult to infer that the rauding process was executed. This is because very short passages might be memorized, and on very long ones it might be difficult to get the individual to persist in executing the rauding process unless there are good motivation conditions present. If the individual is not a very good rauder, $G_a = 4$ or lower, or is an extremely good rauder $G_a = 16$ or higher, then it may also be more difficult to fix conditions so that it is likely that the rauding process will occur just because most situations are typically designed to cater to the kind of rauders that are more frequently encountered.

Reading researchers who are investigating how words or sentences are memorized should take note that what they find in this situation does not necessarily hold for rauding. Reading researchers who are investigating what facts are recalled about a passage that has been studied for a time period that is much longer than that required for rauding should remember to justify their contention that their results will generalize to rauding. Reading researchers who are investigating what can be recalled about a passage that was presented with the admonition to "read quickly but try to remember what you read" should recognize that this instruction is likely to result in skimming, and the results will not necessarily generalize to rauding. Reading researchers who present words, phrases, and sentences for milliseconds of time should remember that they are likely to induce a scanning process, and the results of this research could easily have little or no import for rauding.

Of course, it is possible to design a study to reflect upon the rauding process by setting up conditions that are more favorable to the execution of the memorizing process, just as it is possible to infer something about oxygen by studying nitrogen and contrasting it with oxygen. Yet, there is not much you can learn about oxygen by investigating nitrogen, and there is not much you can learn about the rauding process by investigating the memorizing process or the studying process.

Fran: From what you have told me, it would seem to me that, at a minimum, a reading researcher who was studying rauding should try to measure, and report, the relevant G_a and G_d values.

Carver: Yes, a description of the group in terms of the means and standard deviations of G_a would be desirable, as well as a comparable description of the difficulty of the passages used. Furthermore, passage length, in standard length sentences or standard length words, and rates as measured in Wpm or Spm should be reported. This kind of basic information about the individuals and the passages would be desirable for any reading research whether it deals with rauding or not.

Oh, I almost forgot. Many times a group varies considerably in G_a so it would be helpful to present the results for various levels of G_a or L_a.

Fran: You have been talking mainly in generalities about the implications of rauding theory for reading research. Could you illustrate some of your points by using actual research studies?

Carver: Yes, I could do that in a variety of areas — text structure research, schema research, reading model research, psycholinquistic research, and eye movement research. I'll start with the text structure research of Bonnie Meyer.[1] She has

---

1. Bonnie J. F. Meyer, *The Organization of Prose and Its Effects upon Memory* (Amsterdam, North-Holland Publishing Co., 1975).

reported a lengthy piece of research, which she interprets as indicating that information that is located high in the content structure of a passage is recalled much better than when the same information is located low in the content structure of the passage. Some reading researchers will use this result, or one of a similar vein, to depreciate the importance of rauding theory. These researchers will point out that rauding theory cannot explain this result and would not predict this result. Therefore, they feel that rauding theory is less than adequate.

Let's dig into the details of this situation. First of all, Meyer indicated that the *goal* of her research was to determine whether certain text structure variables could account for certain ideas being recalled from a previous reading of a passage while other ideas are not recalled at all. This way of stating the goal of the research is the first indication that this research is not rauding research at all. To study "recall," suggests at the outset that this research probably involves studying processes rather than rauding processes.

Meyer goes on to tell us what she means by the "structure of a passage." She says that it depicts the relationships among the content of the passage — the structure shows how the author has organized his/her ideas to convey his/her message. These words have a great deal of commonality with what I said earlier about the author writing the sentences of a passage to communicate his/her thoughts. Meyer says she wants to study how the organization of these thoughts or ideas by the author affects how they are recalled later by someone who has read them. From the standpoint of rauding theory, it would be an interesting research project to investigate whether ideas that were high in hierarchy of content structure were recalled better than ideas that were low in the structure after the rauding process has been executed on a passage.

Fran: I thought that was what she did study!

Carver: No, and this is a crucial point! She did not set up her experimental situation so that it is reasonable to infer that the rauding process was executed. Instead, it is more reasonable to infer that her research involved the effect of ideas low and high in the content structure upon what was recalled *after a studying process had operated.*

Fran: Did she tell her subjects in the experiment to "study" the passages?

Carver: No, she didn't. She told her subjects, who were college students, to read the passage at their "normal" reading rate.

Fran: Aren't you digging yourself a hole? These instructions sound just exactly like what you would recommend for inducing the operation of the rauding process.

Carver: They are, but, the catch comes later. Instructions to "read normally" would be expected to produce rauding in many situations, but such instructions do not guarantee that individuals will operate the rauding process. You have to look at the demand characteristics of the entire experiment. Meyer required her subjects to write down, in sentence form, everything they could remember about each passage that they read. This task is one that is terribly difficult. After one has executed the rauding process once at one's normal rate it is not likely that much could be recalled. This is because there are no steps in the rauding process designed to facilitate free recall. When it comes time to write something down one is likely to be embarrassed by the quantity of writing. Thus, it seems likely that the subjects would study the material, and study in this situation would probably involve a memorizing process that would maximize free recall.

Fran: That is an interesting and reasonable speculation on your part but it is not terribly convincing to me that we can be sure that the subjects were not executing the rauding process exclusively.

Carver: Good point! However, I do have what I think is convincing evidence. Meyer had her subjects record their starting and ending times for each passage and she computed reading rates. She reported the mean reading rate for eight subgroups — the mean rate under eight treatment conditions. These mean rates ranged from 106 to 150 wpm, and the grand mean of these eight mean rates was 126 wpm. Since the typical college student rauds at about 300 Wpm, it seems reasonable to infer that these students did not do what she told them to do —

read the passage at their normal rate. Indeed, it seems much more reasonable to infer that they were studying the passage so as to do well on the type of recall tests that they were taking in this experiment. From my point of view, it is questionable to generalize the results of Meyer's research to a rauding situation.

I'm not through with my analysis of this research. Meyer studied Immediate Free Recall and Delayed Free Recall. Immediate Free Recall is obviously more relevant to what thoughts in the passage were comprehended than Delayed Free Recall because the latter involves a heavy dose of forgetting. Let's look at the Immediate Free Recall scores that are most relevant to her finding that ideas high in the content structure are remembered better than ideas low in the content structure. She used three passages, and the differences between the high and low scores for each of the three passages were as follows: 39 percent − 29 percent = 10 percent; 43 percent − 30 percent = 13 percent; 50 percent − 39 percent = 11 percent. Thus, you can see that the differences in recall between high and low content averaged around 11 percent. If the difference in recall between high and low content is only 11 percent when the subjects were studying — selecting which information in the passage it would be best to concentrate on so as to do better on the recall test — then my guess is that this difference, 11 percent, would have evaporated completely if the subjects had actually "read normally," — operating the rauding process.

Don't fail to get my point here! I am trying to convince you beyond a reasonable doubt that Meyer only got the effect she observed because her subjects were operating processes other than the rauding process. If Meyer would now elect to replicate her study of the effect of low and high structure information on its recall when the subjects only had the time and the inclination to operate the rauding process, I am predicting that there would be a trivial or zero percent difference in the recall scores from high and low content. I'm saying that I can easily extrapolate from Meyer's research and infer that content structure is a *trivial* variable when trying to account for differences in recall after operating the rauding process. Furthermore, if this content variable is trivial in accounting for differences in what is recalled after rauding, then it is probably even more trivial as a variable for accounting for differences in the accuracy, rate, and efficiency of the comprehension that occurs *during* the operation of the rauding process.

Fran: I think you have made a good case for your contention that Meyer was actually investigating processes besides the rauding process. However, it sounds as though you think there is something "wrong" with Meyer's research.

Carver: I'm sorry I gave you that impression, because that is not the way I feel about her research. I am trying to make several points. I want you to see that it is reasonable to infer from her research that the variable that she felt was important, text structure, probably does not have an important effect upon the accuracy or efficiency of rauding. I want you to see that it is perfectly legitimate and worthwhile to do the research Meyer was doing as long as it is recognized that it has implications for studying but not the rauding process.

One of the reasons I tend to get emotional about this research is that rauding theory continues to be criticized, illegitimately, because it does not account for text structure. My guess is that text structure will have a very difficult time accounting for an important part of the variance in recall after studying in real world situations and that it will never be found to be an important determiner of the accuracy of the rauding process in real world situations. Someday, someone may collect data that indicates that the efficiency of the rauding process is affected in an important way by the text structure variables, and then they will have to be accounted for in rauding theory. However, as I see the situation at this point, these variables are just as trivial with respect to rauding as they are important with respect to studying. Possibly, someone will point out to me in the future how wrong I am in my thinking, but until then I will continue to deprecate the importance of text structure for rauding. When someone says that rauding theory does not account for text structure variables, I will continue to become angry because I will continue to interpret this remark as a put-down that has no substance backing it up.

Fran: I didn't realize that text structure was an emotional topic for you, Professor Carver. Are you ready to move on to the next topic?

Carver: Almost. Text structure theory can account for certain recall results, such as Meyer's about low and high structure ideas. Rauding theory cannot account for these data, but it should not be expected to, since it is a theory about the amount of passage comprehension, *not recall.* Rauding theory can account for certain findings associated with the comprehension of passages such as the equivalency of reading and auding and the constancy of rauding rate. Text structure theory cannot account for these findings, but it should not be expected to do so, since it is a theory about the effects of studying not the effects of executing the rauding process.

Fran: I think you have more than made that point, Professor Carver.

Carver: I'll stop then. I'm ready to go to a schema research study. I will not spend as much time on it, because many of the same points are relevant. A recent article in *Cognitive Psychology* by Thorndyke and Hayes-Roth[2] illustrates how schema research is generally irrelevant to rauding. In this particular research study, we get a clue about its irrelevance to rauding when the authors state that they have tested their extension of schema theory in two *prose learning* experiments. When an experiment or a piece of research is described as "prose learning," then it is highly probable that a studying process and a memorizing process were used by the subjects; therefore, the results are not reasonably generalized to the rauding process.

The subjects were told that they should read the material carefully because they would be tested on it later. Notice that there is no ambiguity here. If the subjects have a brain in their head they will interpret "read the material carefully because you will be tested on it later" as meaning that operating the rauding process will probably not be good enough, so they are more likely to operate a studying process and a memorizing process, especially when they were allowed to "read" as their own pace.

---

2. Perry W. Thorndyke, Barbara Hayes-Roth, "The Use of Schema in the Acquisition and Transfer of Knowledge," *Cognitive Psychology, 11(1)*:82-106, 1979.

Future research of this nature would be much cleaner, or clearer, if the word "read" were replaced with the word "study" in the directions. The directions would then be to "study the material carefully because you will be tested on it later" and you should "study" at your own pace. This change in wording would more precisely communicate to the subjects what was expected. Also, researchers would be more apt to restrict the interpretation of the results to the studying process rather than confusing everyone by implicitly suggesting that since it was reading research, the subjects must have been rauding, and therefore the results are generalizable to the rauding process. Such prose learning research would probably be interpreted more correctly if it were labeled as "studying" research and never referred to as "reading" research, unless it was perfectly clear that it was not rauding research.

The things I said before about text structure apply equally well to schema theory. Schema theory can account for certain variations in the recall of prose material for which rauding theory cannot account. However, it is not appropriate to expect rauding theory to account for the findings associated with schema theory research. It is just as off base to expect rauding theory to account for these data, which are a product of processes other than the rauding process, as it would be to expect schema theory to account for data that are a product of the rauding process.

Fran: How can you be sure that schema theory does not want to account for what happens after the rauding process has been executed?

Carver: I can't. I can say that the schema research that I have read so far has been conducted in situations where it is very unreasonable to expect the rauding process to have been executed, and it is very reasonable to expect a studying process or memorizing process to have been executed. I infer that schema theory wants to restrict itself to the recall of information that was stored or learned during studying. If the proponents of schema theory want to extend it to include the comprehension that occurs during rauding, I will applaud their future efforts. So far, however, it appears to me that they have avoided the rauding process. So far, rauding theory and schema theory have been concerned with accounting for the effects of different reading processes; the sooner this soaks in, the better off reading research will be.

I think it might be helpful to elaborate even further upon schema theory, since it seems to be drawing the attention of many reading researchers. We have already seen how certain researchers, such as Meyer, have investigated the organization of the knowledge, or information, that is contained in a text, or passage, and how that organization affects how the knowledge is recalled. The schema researchers are interested in investigating something similar — how the organization of knowledge within the individual affects how the knowledge in the text will be recalled. Both of these groups of researchers often contend that they are investigating comprehension, or the process of comprehension, or the act of comprehension. However, as I said earlier, these researchers would be more accurate if they would only contend that they are interested in recall situations that follow studying. Too often the demand characteristics of the experiment suggest that they are not as interested as one might think in how individuals comprehend sentences in passages.

Schema theory covers a broad range of research areas, reading comprehension being only one recent part of this research. Most schema researchers refer back to Bartlett, 1932,[3] for use of the term "schema." The modern day schema research relevant to reading has roots in psycholinguistic research. I think a short historical review would be helpful.

John D. Bransford, in association with a number of other researchers, was interested in "psycholinguistics" and "linguistic comprehension," and published a study in 1971 of sentence comprehension and recall.[4] At the end of this publication the authors made this statement: "Ultimately we hope to be able to characterize the semantic structures abstracted from exposure to connected discourse, and hence lend some precision to Bartlett's (1932) notions of abstract schemas as *what is learned*." In the

---

3. F. C. Bartlett, *Remembering* (London, Cambridge University Press, 1932).

4. John D. Bransford, Jeffery J. Franks, "The Abstraction of Linguistic Ideas," *Cognitive Psychology*, 2:331-350, 1971.

same year we find Dooling and Lachman[5] saying, "The recall of prose may require reconstruction processes that are mediated by an abstract schema (Bartlett, 1932)." Schema research has proliferated since 1970 and has involved a great many instances where individuals have been asked to read passages. Much of this research has not used "schema" in the title but has been advanced under the rubric of "context" research — contextual" factors affecting comprehension and recall. This research can be summarized by the two following quotations:

> A language is a symbol system that is generally used for the purpose of communication, and the effective use of this symbol system depends on other knowledge available on its users.[6]
>
> The meanings of the individual words in a sentence clearly depend upon the interaction of world knowledge and context . . . more important than structures which are in some sense in a text are knowledge structures the reader brings to the text. We shall call these knowledge structures "schema" following usage that dates to Sir Frederic Bartlett (1932) and Immanuel Kant (1781) before him.[7] (pp. 368-369)

We see that the comprehension of a passage from the standpoint of schema theory involves the integration of new information into what we already know. These ideas should not be difficult for any reading researchers to swallow. Indeed, it is possible to trace almost exactly the same ideas in reading research without reference to Bartlett or Bransford.

In 1921, L. W. Pressey and S. L. Pressey published a research paper in the *Journal of Educational Psychology* (Vol. 12, 25-31) entitled "A Critical Study of the Concept of Silent Reading Ability." In this piece of reading research we find the Presseys making this comment: "It appears, then, that ability in silent reading depends very largely upon the nature of the passage read; a good reader in one type of subject matter may very likely be a poor reader with other material." This 1921 statement may

---

5. James D. Dooling, Roy Lachman, "Effects of Comprehension on Retention of Prose," *Journal of Experimental Psychology, 88:*216-222, 1971.

6. John D. Bransford, Marcia K. Johnson, "Considerations of Some Problems of Comprehension, in W. G. Chase, ed., *Visual Information Processing* (1973).

7. Richard C. Anderson, Ralph E. Reynolds, Diane L. Schallert, Ernest T. Goetz, "Frameworks for Comprehending Discourse," *American Educational Research Journal, 14:*367-382, 1977.

seem to place the emphasis on what is contained in the passage, but that is misleading because the essence of this statement is that what a reader brings to one passage may be quite different from another passage, and this affects what happens to comprehension of the passages. Moving on up to 1938, an article was published in the *Peabody Journal of Education* (Vol. 16, 180-191) by Clifford Woody entitled "Attempts at Measurement of Meaningful Experience as a Factor Conditioning Achievement in Reading." Here are some things that Woody said over forty years ago:

> In the average classroom poor achievement in reading, other than that done by pupils who should be regarded as clinical cases, is conditioned by the pupil's lack of experience connected with the things about which he is reading or by his failure to connect whatever experience he may have had with the material which he is attempting to read. (p. 180)

> Connecting the thing to be read with the reader's background of meaningful experience or building such experience becomes the teacher's major problem in successful instruction in reading. (p. 181)

> The symbols to which the child is asked to respond are merely signposts for experience. (p. 181)

These ideas are quite compatible with modern schema theory as well as rauding theory. Finally, I'd like for you to take a look at something that Jeanne Chall said over thirty years ago in 1947 in the *Educational Research Bulletin* (Vol. 26, No. 9, 225-230):

> The current literature on the teaching of reading emphasizes the importance of experience as a factor in reading ability. Reading experts point out that the meaning a reader gets from a printed page depends upon the meaning he brings to it. (p. 225)

The preceding quote summarizes modern schema theory as it applies to reading, yet it had no direct roots connecting with Bartlett. The statement also succinctly states the rationale underlying the comparison of G_a with G_d to estimate A_r in rauding theory. After Chall has finished reporting her research results, she makes this concluding statement:

> The findings point to the fact that the reading process is, in a sense, a circle. We read in order to gain experience, and yet we get more out of reading if we have more experience. (p. 230)

I've been expounding at length. I hope you have gotten the point that the ideas underlying schema theory and its research studies are neither new to the area of reading nor are they incompatible with rauding theory. It is disconcerting to me when I see rauding theory chastised for seemingly ignoring schema theory. Schema theory may yet make a tremendous impact upon research relevant to rauding. Up to now, however, it is difficult for me to perceive how it has advanced our knowledge about rauding in some way that was not previously known; like most new ideas it is a reinventing of the wheel to a large extent.

Fran: I have appreciated these extra remarks about schema theory. I didn't realize that the fundamental concepts of modern schema theory were articulated by reading researchers thirty, forty, and fifty years ago. That gives me a new perspective on schema theory and how it relates to rauding theory. However, I would like to hear a schema researcher respond to your suggestion that these recent research studies have not contributed anything new to reading.

Carver: I would like to hear that rebuttal myself. Possibly, I've overlooked something crucial.

Before we go on to a different topic I would like to respond to a criticism that Anderson et al. made in that *AERJ* article on schema theory from which I quoted earlier. In that research article it was demonstrated that music education students would interpret an ambiguous article that they read one way while physical education students would interpret the same article another way: what you comprehend depends upon what you bring to the page. In that article, Anderson et al. made an inference about reading process models that is worth focusing on: "The strictly left-to-right, or 'bottom up,' theories of reading comprehension proposed by some (Gough, 1972; LaBerge & Samuels, 1974), which involve a linear progression of processing from visual input to an eventual meaning, are not regarded as plausible" (p. 371).

Since some researchers have interpreted rauding theory as being "print driven" it gets automatically classified as not being plausible, as I talked about earlier. I cannot do a good job of defending these models of reading, but my guess is that they *can* be defended from this attack. However, I can defend rauding theory, and I must say I see nothing in it that is not plausible even though it involves a "linear progression of processing from visual input to an eventual meaning." Somehow, some people have gotten the erroneous idea that because rauding involves the perception and articulation of each word in a sequential manner this is incongruent with the idea that prior knowledge, that is, schema, influences how words are recognized and sentences are comprehended. I fail to see any inconsistency here at all.

Fran: Perhaps it will not be long before someone is willing to point out the flaws and inconsistencies in your logic.

Carver: I hope so. It is irritating to me, to say the least, to hear that rauding theory is a "print driven," or a "bottom-up" model and therefore is wrong or "not plausible."

This is as good a time as any for me to tell you, in more detail, my own views on the top-down, bottom-up ideas. I have no problem whatsoever with the general idea that the process of recognizing words during rauding and the process of comprehending sentences during rauding involve both visual input and prior knowledge — both bottom-up and top-down information integration. However, there are certain assertions associated with these ideas that are difficult to swallow given the perspective of rauding theory.

Rummelhart[8] has theorized that individuals use both bottom-up and top-down information integration in what he calls an "interactive" model of reading. His ideas involve a series or treelike structure of hypotheses about the words in sentences; the continual testing of these hypotheses is the substance of the reading comprehension process. He used an example with the two words "the car" at the beginning of a sentence. He showed example hypotheses of five different levels (feature, letter, letter cluster, lexical, and syntactic) in an effort to demonstrate how the reader's knowledge interacts with the visual stimuli to produce comprehension related to these two words. He talks about

---

8. David E. Rummelhart, "Toward an Interactive Model of Reading," Tech. Rep. No. 56 (La Jolla, California, Center for Human Information Processing, University of San Diego, 1976).

parent hypotheses, daughter hypothesis, and sister hypotheses.

From the standpoint of rauding theory, this model may explain and predict certain experimental facts associated with word recognition experiments, such as are involved in tachistoscopic studies. However, such a multihypothesis framework doesn't seem to fit well with what goes on during rauding. During rauding, the phrase "the car" probably would be perceived and internally articulated with only *one* 200 millisecond fixation. To suggest that this process involves one hypothesis is troublesome, but to suggest that it involves multihypotheses is staggering.

Let's analyze a single hypothesis from the perspective of time involved. First, it takes time to construct the hypothesis. Second, information needs to be collected relevant to the hypothesis, and this takes time. Third, the resulting information must be compared to the hypothesis, and this takes time. Fourth, a decision must be made whether the hypothesis is correct or incorrect, and this takes time. Fifth, if the hypothesis happens to be incorrect, steps 1-4 must be repeated, which should approximately double the time. It hardly seems plausible to suggest that all of these steps in the hypothesis testing process can be repeated many times during 200 milliseconds. Instead, these steps may be what occurs when studying isolated phrases, or highly difficult material, or even when trying to read handwriting, a situation mentioned by Rummelhart. However, in these latter situations it is very likely that more than *one* 200 millisecond fixation will be involved.

It seems reasonable that Rummelhart's ideas are descriptive of what goes on during a studying process. However, during the rauding process it is extremely misleading to use the phrase "hypothesis testing" to describe what is going on. Hypothesis testing is misleading, because it suggests the process is somehow tentative and involves all the traditional steps of hypothesis testing. Instead, the rauding process involves very little tentativeness and certainly does not involve all the steps of hypothesis testing. There is obviously a use of prior knowledge or information, which allows one to determine whether "bass" means a fish or a type of sound. Yet, it puts a strain on credibility to say that the rauder of a passage about fishing takes the time to construct a hypothesis that an upcoming word spelled "bass" is probably a fish. In the context of a fishing passage, the letters "bass" mean fish immediately without any hypothesis or second thoughts that it might mean a type of sound. A better word than "hypothesis" in this situation might be "assumption." It is assumed that "bass" means fish in certain contexts, and this implicit assumption will be made without time spent on developing it, or collecting visual information to confirm or deny it. This situation might be likened to other places where these two words "hypothesize" and "assume" are used. If you *assume* that statistical significance testing is a valid technique for use in analyzing data, then you will not spend much time on collecting information that allows you to decide whether this assumption is correct. However, if you *hypothesize* that statistical significance testing is valid, this indicates a more tenuous situation and one that is likely to involve time to test. You might spend much more time reading about statistical significance testing, you might spend time collecting data relevant to its validity, and you might spend a great deal of time struggling with how to interpret the data. All of this time need not be devoted to statistical significance testing if it is *assumed* to be valid. Similarly, during rauding, there appears to be no need to invent the "hypothesis" as a way of modeling the processes that occur.

It is true that sometimes during the operation of the rauding process certain assumptions are made about words and their meanings that are wrong. These errors sometimes are caught because they lead to inconsistent information or incomprehensible sentences. It is true that a rauder might erroneously assume from a 200 millisecond fixation close to the word "commitment" in an article about graduation that the word was "commencement." Ordinarily this type of error would be quite obvious, at least by the time the end of the sentence was reached.

From rauding theory we would say it is not likely that all the steps of a hypothesis testing model could be completed during the time a college student typically spends on the words in a passage. Thus, saying that we *assume* we know what a certain word means in the context of certain passage allows us to cut out a number of time-consuming steps that are proposed from a hypothesis testing framework. Yet, by saying that we assume we know what the word means, I hope you do not get the idea that we can do this with little or no visual information about the word. More precisely, I am saying that college students can handle about six character spaces each 200 millisecond; this is what they need, on the average, to determine the meaning of the word in its context and use the word to reconstruct the thought intended by the author.

Don't forget that I am not saying that Rummelhart's model is wrong in general. I am saying that it may be a good model for attempting to comprehend handwriting where squiggles on a page turn one into a detective who has to consider multiple hypotheses about letters and words to eventually comprehend a sentence. I am saying that it may be an excellent model for one reading process, that is, a studying process. I am also saying that Rummelhart's ideas are not plausible for modeling the rauding process. When one is operating the steps of the highly over-learned rauding process, it is unlikely that one could possibly test all those hypotheses conceived by Rummelhart. I interpret the following statement by A. R. Luria,[9] an eminent brain researcher, as supporting my contention.

> Training or habituation changes the organization of the brain's activity, so that the brain comes to perform accustomed tasks without recourse to the processes of analysis. That is to say, the task may involve a stereotype based on a network of cortical zones quite different from the one that was called on originally when the performance required the help of the analytical apparatus. (p. 78)

I am saying that rauding has become such a highly learned process that it does not encompass all of these analysis steps that Rummelhart calls hypothesis testing with parent, daughter, and sister hypotheses.

I've talked about text structure research, schema research, and reading process models. I'd like to finish up by talking about some eye movement research and a psycholinguistic study that involved eye movements.

---

9. A. R. Luria, "The Functional Organization of the Brain," *Scientific American, 222(3)*:66-78, 1970.

The eye movement study to which I want to draw your attention was conducted by McConkie and Rayner.[10] They used a computerized display to control precisely what was presented to the reader. It was clear that they wanted to investigate the rauding process, even though they did not use that word. Here is what they said: "An important goal for reading research is to develop techniques for studying the processes involved in reading as the person is engaged in the normal reading task, reading a passage for meaning, rather than having to depend so completely on other tasks which are thought to be similar to normal reading in certain ways." They reported upon two studies that are quite complex and difficult to summarize in a few words. Therefore, I will depend upon you to read the methodology for yourself if you are interested. I want to quote at length how they summarized their results. Before I quote them, however, I want to review for you some facets about character spaces and words because they present their results in terms of character spaces.

If we let five letters and one blank space represent a standard length word, and if we assume that a person is fixating upon the center of one standard length word, then it is four character spaces over to the beginning of the next work into the periphery. Look at this picture I am putting on the chalkboard for you. Notice that the second word into the periphery begins ten character spaces away, and the third word into the periphery begins

XXXXX XXXXX XXXXX XXXXX

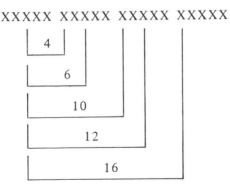

10. George W. McConkie, Keith Rayner, "An On-line Computer Technique for Studying Reading: Identifying the Perceptual Span," *22nd Yearbook of the National Reading Conference* (Boone, North Carolina, The National Reading Conference, 1973).

sixteen character spaces away. Now I'm ready to quote extensively from McConkie and Rayner.

> It appears that different types of information are acquired different
> distances into the periphery, and are used for different purposes. Word
> length pattern information is acquired furthest into the periphery, at
> least 13 or 14 character positions from the fixation point and possibly
> more. This information is probably used primarily for eye guidance.
> Visual shape of words and letters is picked up less far into the
> periphery: the first experiment suggests a maximum of about 10 char-
> acter-positions, and the second indicates that this can be acquired for
> words beginning as far as 10-12 character-positions to the right of the
> fixation point. No evidence was found in either study to indicate that
> word shape is identified further into the periphery than is specific letter
> shape. Finally, the actual identification of word meanings seems to
> occur only for words beginning no further than 4-6 character-positions
> to the right of the fixation point. The reader appears not to make the
> distinction between words and nonwords further into the periphery
> than that.

These two researchers found that during normal reading,
rauders can pick up information about two words away that
might be helpful in guiding the eye as to where the next fixation
point should be located. However, if they are looking at the
middle of one word, they *might* be able to determine the meaning
of the word following the one they are focusing upon. They
would not be able to determine the meaning of the second word
into the periphery. These data are quite compatible with the
contention of rauding theory that each consecutive word is perceived and internally articulated in a word-by-word manner
during a typical reading situation.

With the hindsight of rauding theory, this research report of
McConkie and Rayner's could have been improved by providing
rate information in words per minute or Spm; information
about the values of G_a and G_d would also have been very helpful.

Let's now contrast the McConkie and Rayner research with a
psycholinguistic study done some years ago that involved eye
movement information. In 1967, Mehler, Bever, and Carey
published a study entitled "What We Look at When We Read."[11]

---

11. J. Mehler, T. G. Bever, P. Carey, "What We Look at When We Read," *Perception
and Psychophysics*, 2:213-218, 1967.

They analyzed the linguistic structure of sentences and then studied what parts of the sentence a person fixated upon. They said they found that a person fixates " . . . on the first half of phrase structure constituents" (p. 213). This finding seems counter to rauding theory, which considers eye movements to act simply as a collecting device for perceiving each consecutive word. From rauding theory there is no need to consider the placement of the eye fixations to be important other than that they are moving along allowing each word to be perceived. To suggest that the eye movements during rauding are associated with the meaning or linguistic usage of the words rather than simply where the words are located is anathema to rauding theory.

A closer look at this 1967 research report that superficially seems to refute rauding theory reveals that it was not a study of rauding at all. It was in fact an investigation that could be more properly described as involving the memorization of sentences. The subjects in this research averaged one fixation every .26 letters, whereas a college student rauding at 300 Wpm with an average fixation duration of 200 milliseconds would average one fixation every 5.00 letters. I was able to estimate from the published data that the average rate for the subjects in this experiment was 96 Wpm. To say that this research has something to say about what we look at when we "read" is highly misleading. It has no necessary connection with what we look at when we raud. This is just another example of how muddled things can become in reading research when there is no attempt to separate rauding from the study of other reading processes.

That's it, Fran. I've reached the end of the line. I have no more topics that I want to cover. Do you have any famous last questions?

Fran: No. But, I would like to give you a chance to say something of a parting nature that might leave an indelible impression on me.

Carver: Okay. I'll do two things. First, I want to draw your attention again to the Three Laws of Rauding and the two quantified hypotheses. These three laws and two hypotheses succinctly summarize the essence of rauding theory. Here they are once more for you to ponder and meditate upon.

THREE LAWS OF RAUDING

Law I. Individuals attempt to comprehend thoughts in passages at a constant rate, called the rauding rate, unless they are influenced by situation specific factors to change that rate $(R = R_r)$.

Law II. The efficiency of passage comprehension depends upon the accuracy of passage comprehension and the rate of passage presentation $(E = AR)$.

Law III. The most efficient rate of comprehending thoughts in a passage is the rauding rate (When $R \neq R_r$, then $E < E_r$).

TWO QUANTIFIED HYPOTHESES OF RAUDING THEORY

Hypothesis 3: $\quad A = E_r \dfrac{1}{R}$ when $t \leq t_r$.

Hypothesis 4: $\quad A = \dfrac{1/R}{1/R + i}$ when $t \geq t_r$.

The second thing I want to do is to make a short list of the main points I want you to remember.

1. Henceforth, I hope you will always use the word rauding if you want to refer to a typical or normal reading situation.
2. Scanning, skimming, rauding, studying, and memorizing processes are all different, and don't you forget it.
3. Don't make the mistake of thinking that the results of a reading research study automatically tell you something about rauding or the reading process.
4. Rauding is the most frequently occurring of all the possible reading processes and therefore deserves a great deal more attention than it has received in the past.
5. An individual's rauding rate is constant; it is the most efficient rate of rauding; almost all people raud at their rauding rate; we will do a disservice to most people by suggesting that they should "read" faster because they are likely to become less efficient rauders if they go faster.
6. It is wrong to view typical readers as continually changing their purpose and continually changing their rate; according to rauding theory this conventional view of reading flexibility is wrong.

7. It is right to view typical readers as usually having a single, unchanging purpose and usually having a single, unchanging rate; according to rauding theory this alternative view of "reading" is right.

Fran: Your admonitions sound a little authoritarian, or dogmatic. I'll try to overlook this dimension of your comments and regard what you say as guiding principles.

Carver: I'll accept that. Happy rauding!

LIST OF RAUDING THEORY DEFINITIONS

Accuracy: accuracy of passage comprehension, symbolized as A; proportion of thoughts in a passage comprehended; number of thoughts in a passage that were comprehended during reading or auding per the total number of thoughts in the passage; see Equation 2.

Actual rate: rate of passage presentation, R, when rate is directly manipulated, e.g. by use of motion picture film or time-compressed speech; the rate that accompanies an attempt to directly manipulate the rauding process rate.

Auding: listening to orally presented words, letters, or other language symbols to gain information or knowledge.

Average rate: rate of passage presentation, R, when presentation time is directly manipulated, e.g. by allowing an individual to read a passage for a fixed amount of time; the passage presentation rate that accompanies an attempt to allow the rauding process to proceed at the rauding rate.

Comprehending: understanding or grasping of the meaning of.

Efficiency: efficiency of passage comprehension, symbolized as E; number of comprehended thoughts in a passage per the amount of time allowed for reading or auding; product of accuracy and rate; see Equation 4 and Equation 5.

Inefficiency constant: index of the amount of inefficiency associated with having more than enough time to execute the rauding process once on a passage; symbolized by i; depends upon the rauding rate and the rauding accuracy; see Equation 20.

Memorizing: implementation of those activities which are most likely to result in the recall of information; often involves the word-for-word recall of a passage either in written or oral form; the "memorizing process," as defined elsewhere is the only one of several possible memorizing activities.

Memorizing process: a series of steps carried out on the words of a passage so as to increase the probability that the words can be recalled on a subsequent occasion; see page 19 for an explicit description of a memorizing process.

Operating: carrying out the steps of a process.

Optimal rate: the rate of passage presentation associated with the maximum efficiency of passage comprehension.

Passage: a set of connected thoughts usually in the form of related sentences and sometimes organized in paragraphs; a body of prose material either in spoken or written form.

Presentation time: amount of reading time for a passage, either as allowed or spent depending upon whether time is fixed or variable; symbolized as t; usually measured in minutes.

Process: a series of progressive and independent steps designed to accomplish a goal; a phenomenon that continuously changes with time, usually cyclic or algorithmic in nature.

Rate: rate of passage presentation, symbolized as R; number of thoughts in a passage that are encountered or presented per the amount of time allowed for reading or auding; see Equation 3.

Raud: comprehension of all or almost all of the consecutively encountered thoughts during reading or auding; comprehending 75 percent or more of the thoughts encountered during the operation of the rauding process.

Rauder: one who rauds or attempts to raud; a person who operates the rauding process.

Rauding: attending to words and comprehending each consecutively encountered thought contained in those words; operating the rauding process and comprehending 75 percent or more of the thoughts in a passage.

Rauding ability: the level of passage difficulty at which an individual can comprehend 75 percent of the thoughts; symbolized as G_a when measured in grade equivalents and symbolized as L_a when expressed in school levels.

Rauding accuracy: accuracy of passage comprehension when the rauding process is operated on a passage at the rauding rate; symbolized as A_r.

Rauding difficulty: level of passage difficulty; symbolized as G_d when measured in grade equivalents and L_d when expressed in school levels.

Rauding efficiency: efficiency of passage comprehension when the rauding process is operated on a passage at the rauding rate; symbolized as E_r; see Equation 7.

Rauding process: the process used by an individual to comprehend each consecutively encountered thought. (Note: according to rauding theory, when an individual operates the rauding process on a passage, it involves perceiving and internally articulating each consecutive word in a passage in an attempt to comprehend each consecutive sentence and thereby understand the thoughts in the passage that the author intended to communicate; during reading the rauding process also includes a fixation centered on almost every word in a passage.) See page 18 for an outline of steps in the rauding process that help differentiate it from other reading processes such as those outlined on pages 17-20.

Rauding rate: highest rate at which an individual can raud a passage; maximum rate at which an individual can operate the rauding process on a passage with all or almost all of the consecutively encountered thoughts being comprehended; for passages with rauding difficulty levels below the rauding ability level of the individual, the highest rate at which the passage can be presented and the individual still be able to raud the passage; symbolized as R_r; see Equation 9. (Note: according to rauding theory, rauding rate is also a constant rate, an optimal rate, a threshold rate, and the typical rate at which the rauding process operates.)

Rauding time: amount of time required for an individual to complete a passage while operating the rauding process at the rauding rate; symbolized as t_r; see Equation 10.

Reading: looking at visually presented words, letters, or other language symbols to gain information or knowledge.

Scanning: those receptive processes which involve the intake of information from symbols, often in the form of passages, to determine if that information meets a certain criterion or goal; the "scanning process," defined elsewhere, is only one of several possible scanning activities.

Scanning process: a series of steps carried out on a passage to locate a specific item of information; see page 17 for an explicit description of a scanning process.

Skimming: those receptive processes which involve a sampling of the population of information to learn more about that body of information; involves skipping words when done in connection with passages; the "skimming process," defined elsewhere, is only one of several possible skimming activities.

Skimming process: a series of steps carried out on the words in a passage so as to increase one's general knowledge about the information contained in the passage; involves sampling words or phrases and inferring about what was skipped; see page 18 for an explicit description of a skimming process.

Standard length word: Six character spaces; six consecutive characters including letters, punctuation marks, and blank spaces when the passage is typed; symbolized as W.

Standard length sentence: 100 character spaces; sixteen and two-thirds standard length words; symbolized as S.

Sentences per minute (Spm): rate determined from a count of the number of standard length sentences in a passage divided by presentation time in minutes.

Studying: receptive activities such as a scanning process, a skimming process, a rauding process, a studying process, and a memorizing process, or productive activities such as notetaking, underlining, reciting, and outlining, which are used as part of a strategy for increasing one's understanding or future recall of the information in a passage; reading usually accompanied by certain productive activities that may be referred to as study skills; the studying process, defined elsewhere, is only one of several studying activities.

Studying process: a series of steps carried out on the words in a passage so as to increase the probability that the passage can be rauded; see page 19 for an explicit description of a studying process.

Thought: a hypothetical construct that refers to a unit of information usually expressed in the form of language; corresponds roughly to a sentence or independent clause when expressed in written or oral form.

Words per minute (wpm): rate determined from a count of the actual number of words in a passage divided by the presentation time.

Words per minute (Wpm): rate determined from a count of the standard length words in a passage divided by the presentation time.

LIST OF RAUDING THEORY ASSUMPTIONS

Assumption 1. Rauding exists.

Assumption 2. Whenever individuals are reading or auding, rauding occurs most frequently.

Assumption 3. The rauding process exists.

Assumption 4. The rauding process is the predominantly occurring type of reading process.

Assumption 5. Most individuals behave in the most efficient way.

Appendix C

LIST OF SEVEN RAUDING THEORY PRINCIPLES

Principle 1. Word-for-word. During the rauding process, each consecutive word in the sentences of a passage is perceived and used to try to formulate the thoughts the author intended to communicate.

Principle 2. Subvocalization. Each consecutive word in a passage is internally articulated during the operation of the rauding process.

Principle 3. Sentences. The attempt to comprehend the complete thought contained in each consecutive sentence of a passage is a primary function of the rauding process.

Principle 4. Eye Fixations. An eye fixation is centered upon almost every word in a passage during the operation of the rauding process.

Principle 5. Internal Articulation Rate. There is a certain fastest rate, in syllables per minute, at which an individual can internally articulate all the words and still be able to comprehend each consecutive thought.

Principle 6. Eye Movements. During reading, when the eyes are moved at a constant rate for many hours, they become habituated at this rate.

Principle 7. Accuracy. Rauding accuracy depends upon rauding difficulty and rauding ability.

LIST OF THREE RAUDING THEORY LAWS

Law I. Individuals attempt to comprehend thoughts in passages at a constant rate, called the rauding rate, unless they are influenced by situation specific factors to change that rate $(R = R_r)$.

Law II. The efficiency of passage comprehension depends upon the accuracy of passage comprehension and the rate of passage presentation $(E = AR)$.

Law III. The most efficient rate of comprehending thoughts in a passage is the rauding rate. (When $R = R_r$, $E_{max} = E_r$, or when $R \neq R_r$, $E < E_r$.)

LIST OF FOUR RAUDING THEORY HYPOTHESES

Hypothesis 1. Ordinarily, individuals will read at a constant rate even when the passages vary considerably in difficulty, as long as the rauding difficulty of the passages does not exceed the rauding ability of the individuals.

Hypothesis 2. The optimal rate for comprehending thoughts while reading equals the optimal rate while auding.

Hypothesis 3. The accuracy with which an individual comprehends a passage is equal to the product of the individual's rauding accuracy, rauding rate, and the amount of time per thought presented, provided that the average rate is greater than or equal to the rauding rate.

Hypothesis 4. The amount of time allowed per thought comprehended is equal to the amount of time allowed per thought presented plus a constant.

Appendix F

LIST OF RAUDING THEORY SYMBOLS

A : accuracy; accuracy of passage comprehension: T_c/T_p

$\bar{A}$: estimated accuracy; empirical measure of A that is relatively unbiased; estimates of A not in need of rescaling or $\tilde{A}$ values that have been rescaled

$\tilde{A}$: estimated accuracy; empirical measure of A that is possibly biased; estimate of A that probably needs to be rescaled into $\bar{A}$ values before they can be considered as valid estimates of A

$\hat{A}$: estimated accuracy; empirical estimate of A values derived from the substitution of $\tilde{A}_r$ and $\tilde{R}_r$ values into a theoretical equation and solving for A

A_r : rauding accuracy

$\tilde{A}_r$: estimated rauding accuracy; empirical measure of the value of A_r; may be estimated from $\tilde{G}_a - \tilde{G}_d$ using certain empirical tables; may be estimated from certain curve fitting techniques applied to $\tilde{A}$ values

E : efficiency; efficiency of passage comprehension: T_c/t

$\tilde{E}$: estimated efficiency; empirical measure of E

E_r : rauding efficiency

$\tilde{E}_r$: estimated rauding efficiency; empirical measure of E_r

$E_{\max}$: highest or maximum efficiency

G_a : rauding ability level expressed in grade equivalents; attribute of an individual scaled in terms of passage difficulty, G_d

$\tilde{G}_a$: estimated rauding ability level in grade equivalents; empirical measure of the value of G_a; may be determined from a standardized reading test scaled in grade equivalents

G_d : rauding difficulty level; attribute of a passage scaled in grade equivalents

$\tilde{G}_d$: estimated rauding difficulty level; property of a passage usually determined by an empirical technique that scales

		the readability of a passage, such as a readability formula
i	:	inefficiency constant; calculated from a formula; only relevant when $t \geq t_r$
$\tilde{\imath}$	:	estimated inefficiency constant; determined from $\tilde{A}_r$ and $\tilde{R}_r$
L_a	:	rauding ability level, expressed in the following school levels: primary, Level 1 (G_a = 1-3)/ intermediate, Level 2 (G_a = 4-6)/ junior high, Level 3 (G_a = 7-9); high school, Level 4 (G_a = 10-12)/ college, Level 5 (G_a = 13-15)/ graduate, Level 6 (G_a = 16-18)
$\tilde{L}_a$	:	estimated rauding ability level; usually derived from $\tilde{G}_a$
L_d	:	rauding difficulty level, expressed in the same school levels as described for L_a
$\tilde{L}_d$	:	estimated rauding difficulty level; usually derived from $\tilde{G}_d$
R	:	rate; rate of passage presentation often expressed in thoughts per minute: T_p/t
$\tilde{R}$	:	estimated rate; often expressed in standard length sentences per minute, Spm, or standard length words per minute, Wpm.
R_r	:	rauding rate
$\tilde{R}_r$	:	estimated rauding rate; empirical measure of R_r; expressed in thoughts per minute, standard length sentences per minute (Spm), or standard length words per minute (Wpm)
s	:	the number of actual sentences in a passage
S	:	the number of standard length sentences in a passage; 16.7 standard length words
t	:	presentation time
$\tilde{t}$	:	estimated presentation time; empirical measure of t; usually measured in minutes; a timing of how long the individual was exposed to the passage
t_r	:	rauding time
$\tilde{t}_r$	:	estimated rauding time; empirical measure of t_r; estimated by timing how long it takes for an individual to raud a passage
T_c	:	number of comprehended thoughts in a passage
$\tilde{T}_c$	:	estimated number of comprehended thoughts in a pas-

sage; empirical measure of T_c; often determined by multiplying $\bar{A}$ by $\tilde{T}_p$

T_p : total number of thoughts in a passage

$\tilde{T}_p$: estimated number of thoughts in a passage, empirical measure of T_p; usually estimated by counting the number of standard length sentences in a passage, S

w_p : number of actual words in a passage

W_p : number of standard length words in a passage

Appendix G

LIST OF THE MOST IMPORTANT RAUDING THEORY EQUATIONS

205

(20) $i = \dfrac{1}{R_r}\left(\dfrac{1}{A_r} - 1\right)$ 86

(26) $\dfrac{T_c}{T_p} \cong \dfrac{s_c}{s_p}$ 105

(27) $\bar{A} = \dfrac{s_c}{s_p}$ 105

(32) $\bar{R} \cong \dfrac{S_p}{t}$ 112

(33) $\dfrac{T_p}{t} \cong \dfrac{S_p}{t}$ 112

(34) $\bar{R}_r \cong \dfrac{S_p}{t}$ 114

(35) $\text{Wpm} = \text{Spm} \times \dfrac{100}{6}$ 114

(36) $A = b\bar{A} + a$ 119

INDEX

207